Checklist for Life
for Leaders

Presented To:

_____

Presented B

D1124818

_____

Date:

_____

Checklist for Life
for Leaders

Checklist for Life
for Leaders

NELSON BOOKS
A Division of Thomas Nelson Publishers
Since 1798

www.thomasnelson.com

Published in Nashville, Tennessee, by Thomas Nelson, Inc.

Managing Editor: Lila Empson

Manuscript written and prepared by Marcia Ford and Angie Kiesling

Design: Whisner Design Group, Tulsa, Oklahoma

Library of Congress Cataloging-in-Publication Data

Checklist for life for leaders.
     p. cm.
   ISBN 0-7852-6001-3 (pbk.)
    1. Leadership—Religious aspects—Christianity. I. Thomas Nelson Publishers.
BV4597.53.L43C47 2004
248.8'8—dc22
                                          2004015664

Printed in the United States of America

04 05 06 07 08 CJK 5 4 3 2 1

Heart Attitude

I will be open to the possibilities
that God has in store for me.

Table of Contents

Table of Contents Continued

Introduction

Having then gifts differing according to the grace that is given to us, let us use them . . . he who leads, with diligence.

ROMANS 12:6, 8 NKJV

The word *leader* often conjures up images of corporate CEOs or government officials, the "big brass" positions of power and influence. But the fact is, many of you will fill some type of leadership role in your lifetime—perhaps not as high profile as a CEO but with every bit as much influence on the lives you touch. Maybe you lead a Bible study in your home or own a small business with a handful of employees. Your leadership role may require you to coach a Little League baseball team or instill godly principles in a group of rowdy teenagers at your local church. Or perhaps you are that big-brass corporate leader or government official seeking Christ-centered input on your day-to-day leadership journey.

No matter what your title, deep down you know that the decisions you make today could affect the lives of those you lead for a long time—perhaps even for eternity. No wonder the Bible cautions leaders to lead wisely and to become servants rather than iron-fisted rulers. No leadership manual can offer a silver bullet for flawless leadership, but the stories and wisdom found within these pages will point you in the right direction and provide inspiration and real-world ideas for how to lead God's way.

Like other titles in the Checklist for Life series, this book is designed to help you on your journey by grounding you in biblical principles that relate to leadership. To get the most from the book, keep your Bible handy, as well as a notepad and pen to jot down thoughts. After each passage, reflect on the I Will checklist and perform as many of the Things to Do items as you can reasonably accomplish.

Before you begin this leg of the journey, ask God to be with you every step of the way. That's a prayer He will answer. So start reading, dig deep, and commit to be gut-level honest with yourself. You—and those you lead—have everything to gain by it!

He who walks with integrity walks securely, but he who perverts his ways will become known.

Proverbs 10:9 NKJV

[Jesus said:] "Seek first the kingdom of God and His righteousness, and all these things shall be added to you."

Matthew 6:33 NKJV

If any of you lacks wisdom, let him ask of God, who gives to all liberally and without reproach, and it will be given to him.

James 1:5 NKJV

[Paul wrote:] Therefore, my beloved brethren, be steadfast, immovable, always abounding in the work of the Lord, knowing that your labor is not in vain in the Lord.

1 Corinthians 15:58 NKJV

[Jesus said:] "This, however, is not the way it shall be among you. If one of you wants to be great, you must be the servant of the rest."

Matthew 20:26 GNT

Individual commitment to a group effort—that is what makes a team work, a company work, a society work, a civilization work.

—VINCE LOMBARDI

Checklist for Life *for Leaders*

There is no power on earth that can neutralize the influence of a high, simple, and useful life.
Booker T. Washington

When the solution is simple, God is answering.
Albert Einstein

Relationships

One-on-One

Make my joy complete by being like-minded, having the same love, being one in spirit and purpose.

PHILIPPIANS 2:2 NIV

Jim discovered firsthand just how important relationships are when he hired a new sales force. Now he had a chance to make people his first priority. He took the time to encourage his sales staff, and once a month he recognized and rewarded effort in relevant ways. When he passed people in the hall, he smiled and looked them in the eye rather than looking through them. Performance reviews modeled the "sandwich" approach: layering any negative feedback between positive comments. Before long, focusing on people became second nature to Jim, rather than an item on his to-do list. His company reaped the benefits in satisfied employees and rejuvenated sales. And Jim experienced the priceless feeling of knowing he was respected and well liked for the person he was, not because he signed the paychecks.

Distilled to its essence, the message of Scripture is relationships—your relationship with God and your relationships with others. In fact, Jesus said all the wisdom of the Bible—all the "law and the prophets"—boil down to two great commands: love God and love people. If you do that, everything else falls into place.

How would you rate yourself on the "relationship" scale? Do you see room for improvement, or are relationships naturally your strong suit? People seem to know instinctively whether others like and respect them, or not. Make room in your schedule for "little acts of kindness" to the people you lead on a daily basis. Is someone you work with going through a personal crisis? Let them know you are there for them emotionally, and offer to help in practical ways such as shifting a difficult project to another coworker. Does morale need a boost? Take a five-minute meeting with each of those you lead and point out their strongest on-the-job asset. Jesus related to people as individuals, and as you relate to those you lead not just as employees but as human beings, you'll notice a newfound richness in your organization.

If you look inside any organization and take its "people temperature," you'll get a good idea of how successful that organization is. A company with a high people temperature generates positive word-of-mouth among workers and a feeling of goodwill throughout the organization. Enthusiasm begets performance, and enthusiasm (along with its cousin, goodwill) is contagious. As a leader, if you foster these qualities in your organization you invest for the long haul and increase the value of your premium stock in trade—people.

Relationships are the currency of leadership, for without people—and the necessary give and take that accompanies any worthwhile leadership endeavor—an organization would lose its value and purpose. Since people are your greatest assets, pour your energies into developing them to their fullest potential. Make the people you work with your priority today.

I Will

Realize that my actions mean more than what I say.   _yes_   _no_

Treat others with respect and dignity when they are under my leadership.   _yes_   _no_

Follow Jesus' example of relating to other people as individuals.   _yes_   _no_

Appreciate the differing talents and gifts in each of those who follow my leadership.   _yes_   _no_

Encourage spontaneity and free thinking among those I lead to foster high morale.   _yes_   _no_

Practice little acts of kindness daily.   _yes_   _no_

Look for qualities to emulate among leaders I admire.   _yes_   _no_

Things to Do

☐ Take the "people temperature" of your organization to see how it reflects on your leadership.

☐ Make a short list of individuals who may need extra grace or practical help while going through a personal crisis.

☐ Write down one positive action you can take to improve relations with each person and do it.

☐ Ask two or three colleagues whose leadership style you admire what they do to foster good relationships with their staff.

☐ Read a book on business relationships, such as The 21 Indispensable Qualities of a Leader: Becoming the Person Others Will Want to Follow by John C. Maxwell, and make notes on key truths.

☐ Write down three things you can do to relate better with those you lead.

Things to Remember

Pursue peace with all people, and holiness, without which no one will see the Lord.

HEBREWS 12:14 NKJV

Some friends don't help, but a true friend is closer than your own family.

PROVERBS 18:24 CEV

I [God] led them with cords of human kindness, with ropes of love. I lifted the yoke from their neck and bent down and fed them.

HOSEA 11:4 NCV

Continue to love each other with true Christian love.

HEBREWS 13:1 NLT

If you are nice only to your friends, you are no better than other people. Even those who don't know God are nice to their friends.

MATTHEW 5:47 NCV

Greater love has no one than this, that one lay down his life for his friends.

JOHN 15:13 NASB

Cherish your human connections: your relationships with friends and family.

—BARBARA BUSH

Business is not just doing deals; business is having great products, doing great engineering, and providing tremendous service to customers. Finally, business is a cobweb of human relationships.

—H. ROSS PEROT

Adventure

Fasten Your Seat Belt!

[The Lord said:] "Have I not commanded you? Be strong and of good courage; do not be afraid, nor be dismayed, for the Lord your God is with you wherever you go."

—JOSHUA 1:9 NKJV

Abraham leading his family into an unfamiliar land, Moses leading the children of Israel into an uncharted wilderness, Lewis and Clark leading a small band of explorers into an unexplored West, Neil Armstrong leading other astronauts onto the surface of the moon. And now you— leading your people forward into territory likely to be fraught with surprises, despite all the planning you've done. You're on an adventure, one that can be an exciting and transforming experience.

Adventures take on as many forms as there are people. God has called each person to the sheer adventure of living, an adventure that is unique to each individual. And leadership— well, that's a doubly challenging experience, because with the added responsibility comes added grace and added opportunity.

Leaders use different images to define the journey they are on. One that might resonate with you is the sport of rally racing, which involves a driver—you—who must rely on a support team to navigate a tricky route and arrive at the finish intact. Drivers are in the "lead" position on the team, but they need their codrivers to keep them on course and a service crew to keep everything running smoothly. Drivers also need the right equipment—for instance, seatbelts, which serve as an appropriate metaphor for those things that keep leaders safe and grounded even as they take risks. Think of the common sense and the wisdom God has given you as a seatbelt that keeps you from flying off the handle or acting without restraint when your organization hits a patch of turbulence. They don't diminish the excitement; in fact, they help insure your safety as the adventure unfolds.

Maybe you're having trouble seeing your role as a leader in terms of an exciting quest. If you've had a "crazy" idea for a project nagging at you, it may be time to stop dismissing it and start working on it. Imagine yourself in your current position—but ten, twenty, or even thirty years younger than you are today. What would you do differently? If your organization has been around for a while, think of it as a "start-up" and you as the entrepreneur who started it, also a good idea for someone who operates a franchise or serves in a leadership capacity under *another* leader.

When you catch the vision of your life as an intentional adventure that God has prepared for you, the ride becomes an exhilarating one. Just remember to be strong and of good courage, because God will be with you wherever you go.

I Will

Realize that God has called me to an adventure
and purpose that is uniquely mine.

yes _____ no _____

Help others catch the vision for the adventure God
has placed before us.

yes _____ no _____

Rely on the common sense and wisdom God has
given me to keep me grounded.

yes _____ no _____

Understand that with added responsibility comes
added grace and opportunity.

yes _____ no _____

Remember that God is with me as I lead my team
along the course laid before us.

yes _____ no _____

Think of my role as leader in terms of an exciting
quest.

yes _____ no _____

Things to Do

☐ Choose an "adventurous" image you can relate to (e.g., pioneer,
astronaut) and find a corresponding poster or piece of artwork for
your wall.

☐ Choose a metaphor for yourself as a leader—such as rally car
driver or explorer—and analyze it in terms of the way you lead
your group.

☐ Ask those you lead to in some way depict the team the way they see
it, such as verbally using metaphors or visually through a drawing.

☐ Set a timer for ten minutes and in that time write down all the things
you would change in your organization if you truly saw your mission as
an adventure.

☐ Select an "extreme" project or activity you've been putting off and
begin working on it.

Things to Remember

By faith Abraham, when called to go to a place he would later receive as his inheritance, obeyed and went, even though he did not know where he was going.

HEBREWS 11:8 NIV

I am the LORD your God, who upholds your right hand, who says to you, "Do not fear, I will help you."

ISAIAH 41:13 NASB

O Israel, the LORD who created you says: "Do not be afraid, for I have ransomed you. I have called you by name; you are mine."

ISAIAH 43:1 NLT

[The LORD said to Joshua:] "Never stop reading The Book of the Law he [Moses] gave you. Day and night you must think about what it says. If you obey it completely, you and Israel will be able to take this land."

JOSHUA 1:8 CEV

When Peter saw how strong the wind was, he was afraid and started sinking. "Save me, Lord!" he shouted. Right away, Jesus reached out his hand. He helped Peter up and said, "You surely don't have much faith. Why do you doubt?"

MATTHEW 14:30–31 CEV

It is in the compelling zest of high adventure and of victory, and in creative action, that man finds his supreme joys.

—ANTOINE DE SAINT-EXUPÉRY

The vitality of thought is in adventure. Ideas won't keep. Something must be done about them. When the idea is new, its custodians have fervor, live for it, and if need be, die for it.

—ALFRED NORTH WHITEHEAD

Passion

Holy Fire

[Paul wrote:] Therefore, my beloved brethren, be steadfast,
immovable, always abounding in the work of the Lord,
knowing that your labor is not in vain in the Lord.

—1 CORINTHIANS 15:58 NKJV

Chances are, you are a passionate person. People who become leaders do so in part because of their enthusiasm for their work, for their mission, and for life itself. The air around them seems to crackle with the energy their excitement radiates.

Passion drives your purpose. It's an internal motivation that keeps you going even when there's no tangible reward in sight and no earthly reason to stay the course. It's a fire that burns despite others' attempts to extinguish it.

It's also one of the qualities that defines the apostle Paul. Look at his life: He makes his initial appearance in the Bible as an onlooker at the stoning of the first Christian martyr, Stephen. As a zealous Pharisee, Paul—then known as Saul—vehemently opposed this Jewish sect that was following the teachings of Jesus. Then, as he headed for Damascus in hot pursuit of the believers there, the Lord appeared to him in such a dramatic way that Saul's life was forever changed.

The passion Saul had for persecuting Christians was also transformed—into the passion that Paul, as he was later called, had for Jesus and the truth He revealed. Look at his life after his conversion: His zeal for the teachings of Christ consumed him. He dedicated the rest of his life to passing those teachings along to others, preaching and teaching in and around Jerusalem and spreading the gospel throughout the entire Mediterranean region.

Paul's passion for his life's work was evident to everyone who came in contact with him. If you are by nature a somewhat reserved person, others may not sense your enthusiasm. But there have probably been times when you were so excited about your work that you became more animated and lively the more you talked about it. Try expressing that level of passion in the context of a larger group, even if it's just two or three people.

Stifle the inner urge to curb your enthusiasm. Relax the muscles in your face and let your bright smile and shining eyes radiate the joy you feel within. Let your hands and arms get into the act as well and use gestures to convey your emotions. If any of this feels forced, don't do it; it will only make you miserable and the people around you uncomfortable.

Sometimes all it takes to pass your passion along to others is giving yourself permission to openly express the passion you feel inside. Your enthusiasm will help provide the energy you'll need to persevere in making your vision become a reality.

I Will

Be passionate about the work I do.

yes ___ _no_ ___

Have genuine concern for the people I lead.

yes ___ _no_ ___

Express my enthusiasm for what I do.

yes ___ _no_ ___

Keep external forces from robbing me of my passion.

yes ___ _no_ ___

Learn how to let others recognize my passion for my work.

yes ___ _no_ ___

Realize that I am striving to make a difference in the world.

yes ___ _no_ ___

Encourage others to express enthusiasm for what they do.

yes ___ _no_ ___

Things to Do

☐ _Read about Paul's conversion in the book of Acts to see how God can use passion._

☐ _Write down your own answer to the question in the Lyn St. James quotation on page 27 and elaborate on it._

☐ _Read a short biography or watch one of several good films about Saint Joan of Arc, whose passion for God inspired an entire nation._

☐ _Consider how the teachings of Jesus consumed Paul and gauge your own passion for those teachings._

☐ _Think of at least three people whose passion had a positive effect on you and determine what you could learn from them._

☐ _Come up with several creative and tangible ways you could pass your enthusiasm along to others (by recording an inspiring message, for example)._

Things to Remember

With a leap he [the lame man] stood upright and began to walk; and he entered the temple with them, walking and leaping and praising God.

ACTS 3:8 NASB

[The LORD said:] "So shall My word be that goes forth from My mouth; it shall not return to Me void, but it shall accomplish what I please, and it shall prosper in the thing for which I sent it."

ISAIAH 55:11 NKJV

[Jesus said:] "These things I have spoken to you, that My joy may remain in you, and that your joy may be full."

JOHN 15:11 NKJV

[The LORD said:] "The Sun of Righteousness will rise with healing in his wings for you people who fear my name. You will go out and leap like calves let out of a stall."

MALACHI 4:2 GOD'S WORD

[David wrote:] I call out at the top of my lungs, "GOD! Answer! I'll do whatever you say."

PSALM 119:145 THE MESSAGE

Let all who run to you for protection always sing joyful songs. Provide shelter for those who truly love you and let them rejoice.

PSALM 5:11 CEV

> Whenever I get to a low point, I go back to the basics. I ask myself, "Why am I doing this?" It comes down to passion.
>
> —LYN ST. JAMES

> If you follow your bliss, doors will open for you that wouldn't have opened for anyone else.
>
> —JOSEPH CAMPBELL

Influence

Look Who's Watching

[Jesus] said to them, "Go into all the world and preach the gospel to all creation."

—Mark 16:15 NASB

One name continually rises to the top of the most-influential list—that of Oprah Winfrey. She integrates the positive elements of influence, such as inspiration, vision, and credibility, into her daily television program and has helped shape the thinking of millions of people. She has become the top opinion leader in the country today.

Winfrey's influence did not stem from her position of leadership in a company or organization; her corporate and organizational leadership today stems instead from the influence she already had on American society through her media exposure. She's a powerful example of the importance of influence.

Influence is such an integral part of directing others that John C. Maxwell has gone so far as to say that leadership *is* influence. In one respect, everyone—leader and follower alike—is an influencer, for good or for bad. But a leader's influence is more extensive and carries greater immediate consequences as a result. Your responsibility is to make sure you are an influencer for good, whether you lead a group of five or a ministry of five thousand.

By Maxwell's definition, if you aren't influencing others, you aren't leading, no matter what the sign on your door or the welcome message on your Web site indicates. Genuine leaders have a group of followers who have willingly placed themselves under the influence of the leader. Bosses, for example, may think of themselves as leaders—and many are—but in some cases their "followers" only follow because they have to, and they resist their bosses' influence as much as possible. That's not a picture of true leadership.

True leadership occurs when your life, your wisdom, and your expertise "flow in" to the lives of your followers—an image taken from the literal meaning of the Latin word *influere*. Because your leadership position naturally places you in a more visible role, you need to make sure that what flows from you into the lives of your followers will produce positive results.

You also need to realize that your influence over your followers extends beyond their formal interaction with you. In other words, if you head up a missions organization, for example, you influence your followers—and others—outside of work, as they observe the way you conduct yourself in the community, in church, and with your own family.

Remember, too, that influencers are also influenced by

others. Look closely at the lives of those people who have an influence on you. Are their moral standards compatible with yours? Can you vouch for their character? Have they misused their influence in any way? A person who places a high value on integrity can all too easily come under the influence of a less-than-honorable leader if they are not vigilant.

If you want to get an idea of how you rate as a leader, look no further than your followers. It's partially your influence that has shaped them into what they are right now. They may not be where you would like them to be, but if they are on the right path, then you've influenced them for good. If they're far off the path they should be on, you need to take a good hard look at the influence you are having on them—and the people who are influencing you.

You may never be as influential as Oprah Winfrey, but you will also never know how influential you have been over the course of your lifetime. Even if the population in your sphere of influence totals far less than Winfrey's millions, you are no less responsible for what flows from you and into the lives of your followers, however small their numbers may be. Make sure that what is inside of you is a reflection of the nature and character of Jesus. Then, whether you are imparting knowledge or training or wisdom, you can be assured that the influence you exert is a positive one.

I Will

Remember that what is inside me is flowing into the lives of others.   *yes*   *no*

Make sure my influence on others is a positive one.   *yes*   *no*

Be careful about who is influencing me.   *yes*   *no*

Realize that the quality of my followers is partially a reflection of my leadership ability.   *yes*   *no*

Be aware that my sphere of influence extends beyond the arena in which I am a leader.   *yes*   *no*

Strive to become more like Jesus.   *yes*   *no*

Things to Do

☐ *Read or skim through* Clout: Tapping Spiritual Wisdom to Become a Person of Influence *by business experts Stephen R. Graves and Thomas G. Addington.*

☐ *Schedule regular meetings with an influential person in your organization, either to train or to learn from.*

☐ *Read how one person's influence spared thousands of people in the book of Esther.*

☐ *Analyze the qualities of a successful opinion leader to determine where your ability to influence might be weak.*

☐ *Using your team's willingness to follow you as a standard, determine how you rate as a leader of influence.*

☐ *Examine the way your leadership example has flowed into the lives of others.*

Things to Remember

Let no one despise your youth, but be an example to the believers in word, in conduct, in love, in spirit, in faith, in purity.

1 TIMOTHY 4:12 NKJV

Be prepared. You're up against far more than you can handle on your own. Take all the help you can get, every weapon God has issued, so that when it's all over but the shouting you'll still be on your feet.

EPHESIANS 6:13 THE MESSAGE

My friends, I want you to follow my example and learn from others who closely follow the example we set for you.
Philippians 3:17 CEV

Your word is a lamp to my feet and a light to my path.

PSALM 119:105 NASB

In all things you yourself must be an example of good behavior. Be sincere and serious in your teaching.

TITUS 2:7 GNT

These commands and this teaching are a lamp to light the way ahead of you. The correction of discipline is the way to life.

PROVERBS 6:23 NLT

[Asaph wrote:] Give ear, O my people, to my law; incline your ears to the words of my mouth.

PSALM 78:1 NKJV

They [the righteous] give generously to those in need. Their good deeds will never be forgotten. They will have influence and honor.

PSALM 112:9 NLT

The LORD replied, "If you return to me, I will restore you so you can continue to serve me. If you speak words that are worthy, you will be my spokesman. You are to influence them; do not let them influence you!

JEREMIAH 15:19 NLT

Dear friend, don't let this bad example influence you. Follow only what is good. Remember that those who do good prove that they are God's children, and those who do evil prove that they do not know God.

3 JOHN 1:11 NLT

God, for your sake, help me! Use your influence to clear me.

PSALM 54:1 THE MESSAGE

A lot of them became believers, including many Greeks who were prominent in the community, women and men of influence.

ACTS 17:12 THE MESSAGE

Blessed is the influence of one true, loving human soul on another.
—GEORGE ELIOT

There is no power on earth that can neutralize the influence of a high, simple and useful life.
—BOOKER T. WASHINGTON

Creativity

Tapping the Source

Who has known the mind of the LORD, that he will instruct Him? But we have the mind of Christ.

—1 CORINTHIANS 2:16 NASB

If the word *creativity* makes you think of watercolors or poetry, you need to expand your frame of reference. Creativity applies to every area of life, not just the arts. That includes your role as a leader and the kind of innovative thinking that you contribute to your organization.

Look at the example left by the most innovative leader in history. Jesus transformed religious thinking by emphasizing a relationship with God over adherence to a set of rules. He also transformed interpersonal relationships by teaching His followers to do outrageous things like turning the other cheek and learning to be the servant of others and loving their enemies. Talk about thinking outside the box!

Jesus was the most nontraditional thinker ever—and the Bible says you have the mind of Christ. That sounds like a pretty solid foundation for creative thinking. Like Jesus, you can take conventional wisdom and turn it upside down to transform your organization and the people you lead.

Many successful leaders attest to the value of questioning

the way things had always been done in their organizations; their questioning led to innovative changes that revitalized their vision and energized their employees. Others have found success by approaching a problem in exactly the opposite way from the way the majority approached it; they produced innovation through paradox, much like Jesus did.

Even if you feel that thinking outside the box is not one of your strengths, there's a lot you can do to promote innovation among those you lead. Make sure you create an environment in which creative thinking and innovative action is allowed to flourish. Regularly hold brainstorming sessions in which all participants are encouraged to contribute ideas without fear of judgment or ridicule. Surround yourself with creative thinkers whose judgment you trust—and be willing to take a risk when their suggestions defy conventional thinking.

Creativity can sometimes result in disarray. You will have to adjust to an environment in transition and help your followers do the same. You will likely face opposition from people who are resistant to change, and you will need to be prepared to allay the fears of those who are uncomfortable with the new direction you're heading.

Keep your eyes on the end result, the transformation that your organization has needed. And keep your heart and spirit open to God, who will give you both the peace and the wisdom you will need to allow creative changes to be made.

I Will

Maintain an environment in which innovation is allowed to flourish.

yes _____ _no_ _____

Remember that I have the mind of Christ.

yes _____ _no_ _____

Be prepared to deal with uncertainty among my followers.

yes _____ _no_ _____

Believe that I can be an innovator.

yes _____ _no_ _____

Learn to approach problems from a variety of angles.

yes _____ _no_ _____

Realize that creativity applies to my role as a leader.

yes _____ _no_ _____

Rely on God to see me through times of transition.

yes _____ _no_ _____

Things to Do

☐ _Schedule a brainstorming session to solicit solutions for the most pressing problem in your organization._

☐ _Meditate on what it means to you as a person and as a leader to have the mind of Christ._

☐ _Shake up three routine procedures in your organization by providing creative alternatives._

☐ _Come up with a way to reward innovation and creativity._

☐ _Schedule one-on-one sessions with those you consider to be the most creative thinkers among your followers._

☐ _Bring in a creative person with no connections to your field to observe your organization and make suggestions for change._

Things to Remember

[Paul said:] "In Him we live and move and have our being, as also some of your own poets have said, 'For we are also His offspring.' "

ACTS 17:28 NKJV

My God put the idea into my head that I should gather the nobles, leaders, and people so that they could check their genealogy. I found the book with the genealogy of those who came back the first time. I found the following written in it.

NEHEMIAH 7:5 GOD'S WORD

Each of you must take responsibility for doing the creative best you can with your own life.

GALATIANS 6:5 THE MESSAGE

[Jesus said:] "I want you to be smart in the same way—but for what is right—using every adversity to stimulate you to creative survival, to concentrate your attention on the bare essentials, so you'll live, really live, and not complacently just get by on good behavior."

LUKE 16:9 THE MESSAGE

I'll create praise on their lips: "Perfect peace to those both far and near." "I'll heal them," says the LORD.

ISAIAH 57:19 GOD'S WORD

The things we fear most in organizations—fluctuations, disturbances, imbalances—are the primary sources of creativity.

—MARGARET J. WHEATLEY

Creativity involves breaking out of established patterns in order to look at things in a different way.

—EDWARD DE BONO

Trust

Rock-Bottom Leaders

Those who trust in the LORD are like Mount Zion, which cannot be shaken but endures forever.

—PSALM 125:1 NIV

After years of hard work, Jessica's efforts paid off. Her fledgling cosmetic line had established a small but viable place in the market, making a name for itself as the edgy newcomer with bold packaging and teen appeal. But Jessica realized a disturbing trend: Her trust in the people who worked for her was diminishing with every staff member she added to the company. She remembered the days when it was just her and two trusted friends who ran Making Faces. Now, with twenty-two employees—and the increased chances for employee dishonesty—she felt her trusting nature on the decline. How could she get that trust back? More important, what message was she sending to her workers? She worried that they picked up on the vibe of distrust.

Determined to find answers, Jessica turned to the biblical story of Joseph, who, as second-in-command of Egypt, fostered loyalty through demonstrable shows of faith in his people. When the employees realized how much he trusted them— both to do a good job and to follow an ethical standard—they responded in kind, giving him what he expected. Through

Joseph's inspiring story, Jessica realized a foundational truth: Trust is one of those qualities that runs both ways—you must be willing to trust others, and you must be worthy of others' trust. Without this reciprocal nature, what starts out as a noble instinct dwindles into something with the seed of suspicion embedded in it.

At the next staff meeting, Jessica outlined her expectations for the company and added a compelling closing statement: "Making Faces is only as good as we make it—each one of us. I look around this room and see top-notch people, workers whose creative spark and commitment to excellence have made this company a success. Never forget that your contribution makes a difference."

She created a suggestion box for marketing and productivity ideas, rewarding employees whose ideas got voted "best of show" each month. Next she allowed creative teams to take those ideas all the way from conception to implementation. As Jessica's trust in her people grew, so did their reciprocal trust in her as a leader. It was not anything they said, but rather a nearly tangible essence that pervaded the halls.

Every day as a leader you are called upon to trust and be trusted, whether you verbalize it or not. Like Jessica, make the choice to invest good faith in the people you lead. As you do, your own trustworthiness factor will soar.

I Will

Allow God to give me a trusting spirit. _yes_ _no_

Believe that the people I lead are worthy of
my trust. _yes_ _no_

Remember that trust is a reciprocal trait—I must
trust and be trustworthy. _yes_ _no_

Believe that God is in the business of changing
people for the better, including me. _yes_ _no_

Imagine what my organization would look like
without a foundation of trust. _yes_ _no_

Focus my energies on seeing the cup half full rather
than half empty. _yes_ _no_

Things to Do

☐ *Look for opportunities to stretch your trusting muscle today.*

☐ *Write a good working definition of "trust" and meditate
on it daily.*

☐ *Ask for the trust of those you lead, and be prepared to make
good on it.*

☐ *List three things you could do to foster a trusting environment in your
organization.*

☐ *Think of a mentor or friend who first modeled overwhelming trust in
you and replicate that behavior in your own leadership.*

☐ *Write down one word that best describes your attitude toward trusting
others (such as "tentative" or "growing" and reassess it in six months
with an eye on improvement.*

Things to Remember

Israel saw the great work which the LORD had done in Egypt; so the people feared the LORD, and believed the LORD and His servant Moses.

EXODUS 14:31 NKJV

Offer the sacrifices of righteousness, and trust in the LORD.

PSALM 4:5 NASB

I've thrown myself headlong into your arms—I'm celebrating your rescue.

PSALM 13:5 THE MESSAGE

Trust in the LORD with all your heart, and lean not on your own understanding.

PROVERBS 3:5 NKJV

The LORD is good. He protects those who trust him in times of trouble.

NAHUM 1:7 CEV

Some trust in chariots, others in horses, but we trust the LORD our God.

PSALM 20:7 NCV

All that I have seen teaches me to trust the Creator for all I have not seen.

—RALPH WALDO EMERSON

Someone who thinks the world is always cheating him is right. He is missing that wonderful feeling of trust in someone or something.

—ANDREW V. MADSON

Character

Inside Out

We also rejoice in our sufferings, because we know that suffering produces perseverance; perseverance, character; and character, hope.

—ROMANS 5:3–5 NIV

No one can accuse the Bible of bland imagery. For example, the book of Proverbs likens a beautiful woman who lacks discretion to a pig with a gold ring in its snout. A similar sentiment could be claimed of the leader who lacks character. Without the bedrock trait of character, leaders may achieve success, wealth, and even fame, but they will never gain the respect of those they lead. Instead, their lack of character will most likely be "shouted from the housetops" sooner or later through an action that showcases their true nature, or through the slow decline of characterless years.

In contrast, the leader of character exudes strength, trust, dependability, and a host of other good traits. Though modern culture permits a *laissez-faire* attitude in most things, it demands character of leaders and shows disdain for those who lack it. This is evident in the nation's reaction to headlines of immorality scandals among leading politicians—especially presidents. And once respect is lost, it's much more difficult to win back because respect is something that must be earned. Respect can never successfully be demanded.

Jesus, the ultimate leader of character, told a parable during His most famous speech, the Sermon on the Mount. Using the metaphor of building a house, He likened a foolish man to one who builds his house on sand. When the winds and rain come, pummeling the house with fury, the house falls into a dismal heap. All the man's efforts are wasted because he built on a poor foundation. The wise man, however, is like one who builds a house on a foundation of solid rock. The storms beat against the house but then pass on by, leaving the house standing firm. Because the man took the time to build carefully and wisely, he is able to enjoy the fruit of his labor.

Perhaps character is even more noticeable when backlit by persecution. In the early 1500s a German monk-priest rose to prominence on the world political and religious scene when he opposed the commonly held practice of paying indulgences to the Roman Catholic Church. Through the clink of a few coins and a repeated prayer, faithful Christians were promised that they or their loved ones would be spared in the afterlife. Martin Luther recognized corruption and spoke out about it— forcefully. His stand of conscience and show of character caught the imagination of the common people and made him an enemy of the organized church, as well as key political leaders of his day. When asked to recant his scathing indictments against the church, he said: "I cannot and will not recant anything, for to go against conscience is neither right nor safe. Here I stand, I can do no other, so help me God." Luther's stand sparked the Protestant Reformation.

No book contains more wisdom about building a life of

character than the Bible. The foundation for all true character is a mind and heart set on God. The apostle Paul referred to this when he wrote to the church at Rome, urging them to "rejoice in hope of the glory of God" (Romans 5:2 NKJV). His next statement leaves no doubt that character is gained through hardship and perseverance—two things that carry reward in the long run. The apostle James said it even more bluntly: "Consider it pure joy, my brothers, whenever you face trials of many kinds, because you know that the testing of your faith develops perseverance. Perseverance must finish its work so that you may be mature and complete, not lacking anything" (James 1:2–4 NIV).

But who wants to embrace hardship? Trials and setbacks will never find their way onto your to-do list, yet they are the means by which God takes you from a person of intention to a person of character. As a leader, learn to view every hardship through the lens of faith, with an eye toward your character growth and the big-picture purposes of God. Realize that at times your commitment to character will require you to make unpopular decisions.

What character issues do you face today? If decisions are hanging in the balance that could go either way, choose the path your conscience tells you to choose. Like Martin Luther, your stand for righteousness may not make you popular in the short term, but you will never regret the choices you make for integrity. Allow your character to shine brightly for all to see. As a leader of character, you just may spur others to emulate your behavior.

I Will

Remember that character is something that takes years to build but can be lost in a moment.

yes _____ no _____

Reflect on what it means to be a leader of character.

yes _____ no _____

Look for good character traits in those I lead: integrity, honesty, perseverance, and hope.

yes _____ no _____

Think about what kind of character legacy I am leaving for those I lead.

yes _____ no _____

Be open to character-growing opportunities.

yes _____ no _____

Prove my character by the way I live.

yes _____ no _____

Things to Do

☐ Read the parable of the wise/foolish builders (Matthew 7:24–27) and reflect on its application to your character.

☐ List three practical things you can do to help build character in yourself today.

☐ Think of a hardship you're going through and how you might persevere through it.

☐ Write down one difficult decision facing you today and jot down what your conscience tells you to do.

☐ Read a book about a leader of strong character who changed his or her sphere of influence. A suggestion: Eat Mor Chikin: Inspire More People by S. Truett Cathy.

☐ Reward integrity and character in those you lead.

Things to Remember

I passed on to you what was most important and what had also been passed on to me—that Christ died for our sins, just as the Scriptures said.

1 CORINTHIANS 15:3 NLT

The righteous should choose his friends carefully, for the way of the wicked leads them astray.

PROVERBS 12:26 NKJV

Happy are those who don't listen to the wicked, who don't go where sinners go, who don't do what evil people do.
Psalm 1:1 NCV

Perseverance must finish its work so that you may be mature and complete, not lacking anything.

JAMES 1:4 NIV

Ointment and perfume delight the heart, and the sweetness of a man's friend gives delight by hearty counsel.

PROVERBS 27:9 NKJV

Everything I will say is true and sincere.

JOB 33:2-3 CEV

Let integrity and uprightness preserve me, for I wait for You.

PSALM 25:21 NKJV

The righteous will never be shaken, but the wicked will not dwell in the land.

PROVERBS 10:30 NASB

Do not my words do good to him that walketh uprightly?

MICAH 2:7 KJV

The way of the just is uprightness; O Most Upright, You weigh the path of the just.

ISAIAH 26:7 NKJV

He's a rich mine of Common Sense for those who live well, a personal bodyguard to the candid and sincere.

PROVERBS 2:7 THE MESSAGE

[A leader must be] hospitable, a lover of what is good, sober-minded, just, holy, self-controlled, holding fast the faithful word as he has been taught, that he may be able, by sound doctrine, both to exhort and convict those who contradict.

TITUS 1:8–9 NKJV

Men of genius are admired, men of wealth are envied, men of power are feared; but only men of character are trusted.

—ARTHUR FRIEDMAN

Great ambition is the passion of a great character. Those endowed with it may perform very good or very bad acts. All depends on the principles which direct them.

—NAPOLEON BONAPARTE

Encouragement

Cheers from the Leader

Being confident of this, that he who began a good work in you will carry it on to completion until the day of Christ Jesus.

—PHILIPPIANS 1:6 NIV

As a leader, your words are powerful. What you say today in the hearing of those you lead could have life-altering ramifications. It is your responsibility to make those words have an impact—for all the right reasons.

Everyone needs a cheerleader, someone who stays with you in life, urges you on, and prompts you to be the best you can be. At the foundation of every great leader is an encouraging heart—the kind that constantly looks for ways to encourage others. As a leader, it is your privileged task to spur on the hearts of the people you lead, energizing them to develop to their fullest potential.

Encouraging those you lead is one of your primary roles. As you cheer your people on, you give them a dose of you-can-do-it when they need it most. You instill confidence by showing you believe in them, even when they don't get it right.

In contrast, consider the leader who only tells people about the things they do wrong. Some leaders make it a habit to lead this way—speaking words that cut deep into the spirit when the deal falls through, or the account is lost, or the presentation doesn't go as planned.

People who cheer others on leave an indelible mark in the lives they touch and become the mentors and colleagues whose words of encouragement hold the power to change organizations for the better.

Nearly two thousand years ago, a leader spoke words of encouragement to the people he led, and they still contain the power to ignite hope and belief in those who read them. The apostle Paul wrote to a group of people in the coastal city of Philippi, "I thank my God every time I remember you" and later, "I have you in my heart." Imagine the boldness his words sparked in those who hungrily read his letter. Though he was far away from them geographically at the time, Paul's words possessed the ability to spur the Philippians on to be their best selves. They still echo the same encouragement to people today.

As you take up the mantle of leadership today, remember to infuse your words with encouragement. Praise is always a more powerful motivator than criticism.

I Will

Reflect on the individuals who became the biggest
encouragers in my own life and think of ways to
emulate their behavior.

yes _no_

Look for opportunities to be an encourager today.

yes _no_

Listen to and assess the impact of the words of
other leaders around me.

yes _no_

Create opportunities to encourage others through
my words and actions.

yes _no_

Trust God to bring the people who need
encouragement most across my path.

yes _no_

Model encouragement for the rising leaders in my
group or organization.

yes _no_

Things to Do

☐ *Tell five people something positive about their performance or
personality today.*

☐ *Create a list of people who are undergoing tough times—and need a
special word of encouragement. Call and tell them you appreciate what
they bring to the organization.*

☐ *Launch a recognition program to reward effort, small and big.*

☐ *Network with other leaders who exemplify leaderships of
encouragement and allow their positive examples to rub off on you.*

☐ *Do a mental inventory of how you encouraged someone today.*

☐ *Write a personal encourager mission statement to guide your behavior,
outlining ways you can cheer on the people you lead.*

Things to Remember

[Paul wrote:] We never give up. Our bodies are gradually dying, but we ourselves are being made stronger each day. These little troubles are getting us ready for an eternal glory that will make all our troubles seem like nothing.

2 CORINTHIANS 4:16–17 CEV

Whatever things are true, whatever things are noble, whatever things are just, whatever things are pure, whatever things are lovely, whatever things are of good report, if there is any virtue and if there is anything praiseworthy— meditate on these things.

PHILIPPIANS 4:8 NKJV

[Paul wrote:] Therefore, since we have this ministry, as we have received mercy, we do not lose heart.

2 CORINTHIANS 4:1 NKJV

If ye then be risen with Christ, seek those things which are above, where Christ sitteth on the right hand of God.

COLOSSIANS 3:1 KJV

[Paul wrote:] Now may our Lord Jesus Christ Himself, and our God and Father, who has loved us and given us everlasting consolation and good hope by grace, comfort your hearts and establish you in every good word and work.

2 THESSALONIANS 2:16–17 NKJV

Instruction does much, but encouragement does everything.
—JOHANN WOLFGANG VON GOETHE

Note how good you feel after you have encouraged someone else. No other argument is necessary to suggest that [you] never miss the opportunity to give encouragement.
—GEORGE M. ADAMS

Boldness

Walking on Water

Do not throw away your confidence; it will be richly rewarded.

—HEBREWS 10:35 NIV

The disciples didn't know what to make of the apparition-like image that emerged in the midst of a violent storm on the Sea of Galilee. Believing they were seeing a ghost, they cried out in fear. The image—Jesus—spoke to them, assuring them of who He was and that they had nothing to fear.

Peter alone seemed inclined to believe Him, boldly telling Jesus to prove Himself by commanding him to walk on the water, just as He was doing. Jesus complied, and, full of confidence, Peter did as Jesus commanded. Stepping out of the boat, Peter realized he was walking on the water! But soon enough, the howling wind and raging sea distracted him, and the fear returned. Peter lost his boldness and began to sink. Jesus saved him, but the lesson was clear—Peter lacked the kind of faith it took to see this miracle through to its completion.

Hebrews 10:35 suggests that you will be rewarded as long as you don't do as Peter did and throw away your confidence. Throughout the New Testament in particular, the biblical writers emphasize the boldness and confidence you can have in approaching God and in your own ability to do what He has called you to do.

Leadership requires an authoritative approach to problem solving, decision making, and the everyday challenges that all leaders must face. Each time you act decisively, you build up your confidence, which enables you to act decisively the next time around. Confidence in yourself alone, however, creates the perfect breeding ground for arrogance; confidence in God, and in the abilities He has given you, is the true test of authoritative leadership.

You will have days when you begin to second-guess your decisions and wonder what happened to the boldness you used to feel whenever you were confronted with a particularly difficult challenge. Don't worry—you're still the same person. You may just need to pray a little more and rely on God a little more. Your faltering confidence could serve as a warning sign that you were starting to trust yourself apart from your trust in God.

Remember that you are a representative of God here on earth. Can anything possibly give you more confidence than that? God has entrusted you to be His ambassador to the environment in which you work and live. Let those you lead see you acting with the authority that only a representative of God Himself can command.

I Will

Realize that my confidence, even in myself, must be grounded in my faith in God.

yes   _no_

Hold fast to the confidence I have.

yes   _no_

Act decisively.

yes   _no_

See myself as a representative of God.

yes   _no_

Be alert to the warning signs that I'm beginning to trust myself apart from God.

yes   _no_

Let those I lead see that my confidence comes from God.

yes   _no_

Thank God for giving me the ability to lead with boldness.

yes   _no_

Things to Do

☐ _Read the story of Jesus and Peter walking on the water in Matthew 14._

☐ _Practice giving your next speech or presentation with the boldness of an ambassador of God Himself._

☐ _Rate your performance at the last meeting you conducted in terms of the confidence you exhibited._

☐ _Read a short biography of a leader like Winston Churchill, whose confidence rallied an entire nation that was on the brink of despair._

☐ _The next time the president of the United States gives a televised speech, tape it and analyze his ability to project an authoritative image._

☐ _Use a concordance to look up biblical references to the qualities of boldness and confidence._

Things to Remember

We can go to God with bold confidence through faith in Christ.

EPHESIANS 3:12 GOD'S WORD

[A voice said:] "You, mortal man, must not be afraid of them or of anything they say. They will defy and despise you; it will be like living among scorpions. Still, don't be afraid of those rebels or of anything they say."

EZEKIEL 2:6 GNT

The wicked run away when no one is chasing them, but the godly are as bold as lions.

PROVERBS 28:1 NLT

The LORD will be your confidence and will keep your foot from being caught.

PROVERBS 3:26 NASB

Be of good courage, and He shall strengthen your heart, all you who hope in the LORD.

PSALM 31:24 NKJV

In all these things we overwhelmingly conquer through Him who loved us.

ROMANS 8:37 NASB

Boldness in business is the first, second, and third thing.

—H. G. BOHN

When you cannot make up your mind which of two evenly balanced courses of action you should take, choose the bolder.

—WILLIAM JOSEPH SLIM

Servanthood

A Heart to Serve

[Jesus said:] "This, however, is not the way it shall be among you. If one of you wants to be great, you must be the servant of the rest."

—MATTHEW 20:26 GNT

Leaders who have a heart to serve others—a genuine desire to meet the needs of their followers—in recent decades have come to be known as "servant leaders." Servant leadership involves making the care and development of the people in an organization the leader's primary concern. It's a way of being a leader that existed in Old Testament times, found its ultimate expression in the person of Jesus, and has made a comeback in businesses, churches, and institutions in America and beyond.

The key is developing—and nurturing—a servant's heart, a godly desire to help other people by lightening their load or making their lives better in big and little ways. Leaders who possess a servant's heart are the ones who pitch in to help with the dirty work and the menial tasks and the unpleasant chores *before* everyone is stretched to the limit of endurance. They are the ones who stay late with the rest of the group to make sure a critical mailing gets out on time, the ones who double-check the sound system and help set up the chairs for the evening's big meeting. Most important of all, they are the ones who do it all for real and not for show.

You can develop a servant's heart first of all by asking God to give you a compelling desire to serve others. Study examples of servant leaders in the Bible, starting with Jesus and continuing with people like Moses, who provide clues to finding true servant leaders.

As you read about the biblical models of servant leadership, you'll see that several common characteristics emerge: an attitude of humility, a willingness to listen, an ability to empathize with the needs of others, a commitment to seeing that those needs are met whenever possible, and a gift for instilling a vision for a better future in the lives of those they lead. Be specific in asking God to help you develop those qualities in your own life.

Continue your quest for a servant's heart by looking for little things you can do to help those you lead. The more subtle and unobtrusive your actions are, the more credibility they will carry. Perform acts of service anonymously whenever possible and discover the joy that results. Be on the lookout for examples of servant leadership in the people around you, in articles you read, in stories you hear on the news. Enter the term "servant leadership" in a search engine and explore several Web sites to see how individuals and organizations have transformed their brand of leadership by incorporating into it the concept of servanthood. Learn from those examples, and apply what you learn toward transforming your own leadership style.

Some leaders are reluctant to embrace the concept of servanthood out of fear that it will undermine their authority. But the truth of the matter is that as you serve those you are responsible to lead, your authority will be strengthened. They will see a leader who cares more about people than image, more about getting the job done than about who does it, more about accomplishing the mission than about pulling rank. With all that will come a measure of respect that you would be hard pressed to earn in any other way.

Keep your servant's heart alive and active throughout your lifetime. Countless people have found inspiration and purpose in the example of former President Jimmy Carter, who helps build houses for the underprivileged, teaches Sunday school, and mows the grass at church when he could easily give it all up and rest on his laurels. He's not alone; powerful leaders in all walks of life bear the mark of servanthood in the quiet acts they perform on a daily basis.

You have an opportunity to make a difference in the world around you by expanding your work to include reaching the heart of the people you lead with your own servant's heart. Follow the examples of Jesus, Moses, and other biblical servant leaders. Allowing God to give you a servant's heart, and practicing servanthood each day, will transform your leadership style—as well as your life.

I Will

Ask God to give me a servant's heart. _yes_   _no_

Follow Jesus' example of servant leadership. _yes_   _no_

Be willing to do the kinds of things I ask others to do. _yes_   _no_

Serve God and people with a joyful spirit. _yes_   _no_

Recognize the authority that comes with servant leadership. _yes_   _no_

Expect nothing in return from those I serve. _yes_   _no_

Things to Do

☐ After reading Mark 10:42–45, note how the principle described in the passage can transform your leadership style.

☐ Demonstrate servant leadership in your organization this week by performing a routine or undesirable task normally done by someone else.

☐ Serve your family by secretly doing a chore no one would ever expect you to do. If you're single, apply this to extended family or a friend.

☐ Think of creative ways to serve people "outside" of your organization, such as restaurant workers, and act on it as a way of establishing servanthood as a lifestyle.

☐ Turn the tables on the person whose job it is to help meet your needs (for example, bring him a cup of coffee, handle some of her unpleasant phone calls).

☐ Read any one of the books on servant leadership by Robert K. Greenleaf, who coined the term and popularized the concept.

Things to Remember

[Jesus], being in very nature God, did not consider equality with God something to be grasped, but made himself nothing, taking the very nature of a servant, being made in human likeness.

PHILIPPIANS 2:6–7 NIV

[Paul wrote:] I am free. I don't belong to anyone. But I make myself a slave to everyone. I do it to win as many as I can to Christ.

1 CORINTHIANS 9:19 NIrV

[Jesus said:] "The Son of Man did not come to be served, but to serve, and to give His life a ransom for many."
Mark 10:45 NKJV

[Jesus] said to them, "The kings of the Gentiles lord it over them; and those who have authority over them are called 'Benefactors.' But it is not this way with you, but the one who is the greatest among you must become like the youngest, and the leader like the servant."

LUKE 22:25–26 NASB

[Jesus said:] "Blessed are those servants whom the master finds awake when he comes. I can guarantee this truth: He will change his clothes, make them sit down at the table, and serve them."

LUKE 12:37 GOD'S WORD

Serve the LORD with gladness; come before His presence with singing.

PSALM 100:2 NKJV

[Paul wrote:] Our message is not about ourselves. It is about Jesus Christ as the Lord. We are your servants for his sake.

2 CORINTHIANS 4:5 GOD'S WORD

Then a voice came from the throne, saying, "Praise our God, all you His servants and those who fear Him, both small and great!"

REVELATION 19:5 NKJV

You, brethren, have been called to liberty; only do not use liberty as an opportunity for the flesh, but through love serve one another.

GALATIANS 5:13 NKJV

[Jesus said,] "If anyone serves Me, he must follow Me; and where I am, there My servant will be also; if anyone serves Me, the Father will honor him."

JOHN 12:26 NASB

[Jesus said:] "Who is greater, the one who reclines at the table or the one who serves? Is it not the one who reclines at the table? But I am among you as the one who serves."

LUKE 22:27 NASB

The measure of a man is not the number of his servants, but in the number of people whom he serves.

—PAUL D. MOODY

No leader is worth his salt who won't set up the chairs.

—PETER DRUCKER

Choices

What's Your Line?

I call Heaven and Earth to witness against you today: I place before you Life and Death, Blessing and Curse. Choose life so that you and your children will live.

—Deuteronomy 30:19 THE MESSAGE

Carl studied the spreadsheet one more time before calling it a night. As his tired eyes pored over the figures, he realized he faced a painful decision: either close the East Coast warehouse (and give a modest severance package to the laid-off employees) or trim salaries company-wide. Neither decision would make him popular, but he knew the company couldn't survive without drastic measures.

After consulting with two or three respected business mentors, he made his decision and consciously chose to move forward rather than wallow in what-ifs about the alternate choice. Though difficult, the choice he faced called forth the best in him as a leader because he knew his decision would affect the lives of his employees, not just the bottom line.

Into every life come innumerable choices. If you're a leader, you face choices every day, and deciding what to do about those choices commands much of your time and energy. When to buy, when to staff up, when to downsize, when to move, when to call it quits—all these and other decisions confront you with dizzying regularity. With so many choices, it can be difficult knowing which tack to take. Yet the leadership "gene" is in you to the core, and you thrive on the flux between chaos and structure. Perhaps you can't imagine life lived anywhere but at the helm of your organization.

Wise counsel and the record of past experience play key roles in the decision-making process of the smart leader. But, more than anything, the call of a clear conscience should be your guide. It's been said that a clear conscience is to the mind what health is to the body.

Fifteen hundred years before Christ, Moses led a band of weary people out of captivity toward a goal they'd only dreamed about for years: the elusive promised land. Suddenly, the goal was within their sight. Even better, it was geographically attainable. Yet, curiously, God set before them what seemed to be a no-brainer decision—to choose blessing or a curse, life or death. Though it sounds strange to our postmodern ears, He was asking them in figurative language to trust Him and follow His ways—no matter what befell them. But He left the choice to them.

Though it may not seem that choices of biblical proportions face you today, remember that the God who pointed the way toward the promised land is still in the business of inspiring His people. If you listen for His voice, He will tell you what to do.

I Will

Ask God for wisdom in every decision I make.

yes ___ no ___

Consider the long- and short-range consequences of my choices.

yes ___ no ___

Rely on godly counsel and the wisdom of past experience to guide me.

yes ___ no ___

Think through how my choices will affect those I lead.

yes ___ no ___

Realize that free will is a God-given privilege not to be taken for granted.

yes ___ no ___

Allow God's will to take precedence over my will.

yes ___ no ___

Prepare my heart before every major decision.

yes ___ no ___

Things to Do

☐ *Read a book on making difficult choices, such as* How Good People Make Tough Choices *by Rushworth M. Kidder, and assess your own decision-making ability.*

☐ *Make a list of pros and cons to the decision you're about to make.*

☐ *Make a decision today that you've been putting off, and mentally prepare for the next most urgent decision facing you.*

☐ *Compare decision-making strategies of two mentor/leaders and assess if either would work for you.*

☐ *Transform a bad decision you made in the past into a learning experience by listing how you might have handled it differently today.*

☐ *Watch a movie about a leader who must make tough choices, such as* Hoosiers *or* Dead Poets Society.

Things to Remember

Your ears shall hear a word behind you, saying, "This is the way, walk in it," whenever you turn to the right hand or whenever you turn to the left.

ISAIAH 30:21 NKJV

I will instruct you and teach you in the way you should go; I will counsel you and watch over you.

PSALM 32:8 NIV

The steps of a good man are ordered by the LORD, and He delights in his way.

PSALM 37:23 NKJV

Do not be afraid or discouraged, for the LORD is the one who goes before you. He will be with you; he will neither fail you nor forsake you."

DEUTERONOMY 31:8 NLT

Where there is no counsel, the people fall; but in the multitude of counselors there is safety.

PROVERBS 11:14 NKJV

Prefer my [wisdom's] life—disciplines over chasing after money, and God-knowledge over a lucrative career.

PROVERBS 8:10 THE MESSAGE

Every choice moves us closer to or farther away from something. Where are your choices taking your life? What do your behaviors demonstrate that you are saying yes or no to in life?

—ERIC ALLENBAUGH

As simple as it sounds, we all must try to be the best person we can: by making the best choices, by making the most of the talents we've been given.

—MARY LOU RETTON

Initiative
Seize the Day— and the Moment

I'm glad from the inside out, ecstatic; I've pitched my tent in the land of hope.

—ACTS 2:26 THE MESSAGE

Jack felt his initiative flagging after a particularly hard year. Where was his old drive, that get-up-and-go that fueled his leadership on autopilot in days gone by? After work one day, he vented his frustration to a close friend. Was he washed up as a leader? Should he turn over the reins to a younger, more energetic person?

Jack's friend assured him that every leader goes through hills and valleys—those mountaintop highs of peak performance and the lowland sloughs of despondency and discouragement. He also suggested steps Jack could take to recharge his waning battery, such as scheduling time off to allow his body and mind to become refreshed. He recommended Jack reread the biblical story of David, a leader who achieved success against overwhelming odds. Like David, Jack rose to leadership at a young age and faced obstacles that might have thwarted him at every turn. But David persisted because he maintained a sense of destiny and divine purpose in his calling. Finally, by surrounding himself with passionate people—individuals who see the cup perpetually half full rather than half empty—Jack would be more likely to recapture some of his own enthusiasm, a precursor to initiative.

In defining *initiative*, Webster's uses words like *energy, aptitude, action*, and *enterprise*. No wonder this quality is so coveted by forward-thinking organizations. At its essence, *initiative* is the crude oil of venturing. Everyday opportunities arrive, but it takes the courage of a leader to strike while those opportunities are still hot.

Jack took his friend's advice to heart and made changes in his schedule that allowed him time to reclaim some of his former drive. Once his mind, spirit, and body were reinvigorated, he experienced clarity of thought, a refueled sense of purpose, and the physical strength to carry the heavy load of leadership.

As you go about the task of leadership today, look for those golden moments that are ripe for the taking. Train your best energies on them, and invest time in developing them into the action steps that will move your organization in the direction of success. Is there a project you've been putting off that needs addressing? A difficult account you've wanted to pursue (but lacked the energy due to a flagging spirit)? Now's the time to reset your focus on the things that really matter in your organization.

Two Latin words that have become cliché in our culture still hold the key for true leaders: *carpe diem*, or "seize the day." Always mixed with a dose of risk, initiative will keep your leadership vital. As you take steps to recharge your own battery, your days and moments will be filled with the vibrant initiative that sets leaders apart from followers.

I Will

Learn to recognize opportunities in all their varying forms.

yes _____   _no_ _____

Ask God to restore my spiritual vigor.

yes _____   _no_ _____

Trust that my leadership instinct is alive and well.

yes _____   _no_ _____

Be open to the possibilities that God has in store for me.

yes _____   _no_ _____

Reflect on the meaning of the phrase _carpe diem_.

yes _____   _no_ _____

Thank God for the leadership gift of an enterprising spirit.

yes _____   _no_ _____

Have an attitude of great expectations.

yes _____   _no_ _____

Things to Do

☐ _Write a sentence describing your God-given destiny, as you see it, and post it next to your computer._

☐ _Schedule a getaway to recharge your battery._

☐ _Do a Web search on leadership initiative, and write down at least three takeaway thoughts._

☐ _Seek out the company of visionary, passionate people and network with them at least once a week._

☐ _Think of one opportunity that is hot at the moment and list three or four strategies to bring that opportunity to fruition._

☐ _Read the Old Testament story of David and notice how many times he took initiative in the face of overwhelming odds._

Things to Remember

Whatever you do, do well, for in death, where you are going, there is no working or planning, or knowing, or understanding.

ECCLESIASTES 9:10 TLB

Commit your way to the LORD; trust in him and he will do this.

PSALM 37:5 NIV

I'm not saying that I have this all together, that I have it made. But I am well on my way, reaching out for Christ, who has so wondrously reached out for me.

PHILIPPIANS 3:12 THE MESSAGE

Then Moses called Bezalel and Aholiab, and every gifted artisan in whose heart the LORD had put wisdom, everyone whose heart was stirred, to come and do the work.

EXODUS 36:2 NKJV

The seed on good soil stands for those with a noble and good heart, who hear the word, retain it, and by persevering produce a crop.

LUKE 8:15 NIV

To those who by perseverance in doing good seek for glory and honor and immortality, eternal life.

ROMANS 2:7 NASB

Initiative is doing the right thing without being told.
—VICTOR HUGO

Genius is initiative on fire.
—GEORGE HOLBROOK JACKSON

Honesty

Truth Quest

Dishonest scales are an abomination to the LORD, but a just weight is His delight.

—PROVERBS 11:1 NKJV

With profits down, Bob wondered how he would make ends meet. He knew one of his competitors in the marketplace had resorted to padding the company's year-end reports to boost shareholder investments. But, as a godly leader, Bob committed early in his career never to resort to dishonest means for personal gain. Meanwhile, he faced the very real possibility of going out of business. How would his company survive?

Scandals of dishonest dealings in the corporate world rocked the early twenty-first century, causing leaders everywhere to sit up and take notice. Had they begun bending the rules too, starting down the slippery slope of dishonesty? How about those gray areas where the line between black and white seemed a bit blurry? Would anyone ever really know—or be hurt by a tiny indiscretion? Though the fictional incident with Bob seems trivial compared to the headlined deceit of high-profile companies, seen through God's eyes there's no room for gray areas at all when it comes to honesty.

As a leader, your word is your honor—and your actions are its demonstration. Even when you think no one is watching, someone probably is—and God certainly is. Thousands of years ago King Solomon penned inspired words of wisdom that are still relevant in the business world of today. Market-goers in ancient Israel were wise to the common practice of unscrupulous merchants who put hidden weights in their scales, racking up bigger sales for themselves. Yet they were helpless to change the corrupt system. Instead, they packed up their bundles and headed home with three-quarters of a pound of grain when they paid for a whole pound.

During times of economic downturn it may be tempting to add extra hours to a service invoice or pad the bottom line with funds earmarked for shareholders—or a charitable donation. For every golden rule of upright business practice, humans can find a loophole through it. But when the ledger of life is balanced, who will be found wanting in the honesty category? Instead of padding the books or hiding assets to evade taxes, a leader would do better to find other ways of reducing costs. For example, he could conserve paper napkins and other "throwaway" items that easily get wasted.

Make it your goal to practice honesty in all your dealings, big and small. Not only will you sleep with a clear conscience every night, but that wonderful, inexplicable law of the universe will go into effect for you: Blessing follows integrity as surely as spring follows winter's chill.

I Will

Be my truest self in the presence of others.

yes   *no*

Esteem honesty in the actions of others.

yes   *no*

Make myself vulnerable and transparent to those
I lead.

yes   *no*

Live by the honor code in and out of the workplace.

yes   *no*

Recognize that there's no such thing as a white lie.

Remember that as a leader others are looking to me
to model integrity.

yes   *no*

Trust God to continually make me in His image.

yes   *no*

Things to Do

☐ *Ask God to help you be truthful in your business dealings.*

☐ *Memorize Proverbs 16:10–11.*

☐ *Reward honesty in those you lead—in small but meaningful ways.*

☐ *Take an inventory of your recent business practices and assess your honesty.*

☐ *Study the book of Proverbs for words of truth to apply to your own life.*

☐ *Post the Golden Rule where you can see it easily.*

☐ *Ask a colleague to rate your reputation for honest business dealings in the community.*

Things to Remember

You must stop telling lies. Tell each other the truth, because we all belong to each other in the same body [of Christ].

EPHESIANS 4:25 NCV

Whoever would love life and see good days must keep his tongue from evil and his lips from deceitful speech.

1 PETER 3:10 NIV

But for as long as I draw breath, and for as long as God breathes life into me, I refuse to say one word that isn't true. I refuse to confess to any charge that's false.

JOB 27:3–4 THE MESSAGE

He who works deceit shall not dwell within my house; he who tells lies shall not continue in my presence.

PSALM 101:7 NKJV

Those who are godly hate lies; the wicked come to shame and disgrace.

PROVERBS 13:5 NLT

My honesty will testify for me in the future.

GENESIS 30:33 NIV

Honesty is the cornerstone of all success, without which confidence and ability to perform shall cease to exist.

—MARY KAY ASH

There is no twilight zone of honesty in business. A thing is right or it's wrong. It's black or it's white.

—JOHN F. DODGE

Goals

Setting Your Sights High

There are many plans in a man's heart, nevertheless the
LORD's counsel—that will stand.

—PROVERBS 19:21 NKJV

As you navigate your organization, you fulfill a role not
unlike that of sea captain. Under your command, the ship sets
sail with a prescribed destination—a specific goal—in view,
and the crew follows your lead in reaching it. As you make
headway toward that overriding goal, numerous other
minigoals or destinations must continually be set and met.
Otherwise you would find yourself at the helm of a foundering
ship.

What is it about goal setting that so captures the
imagination of leaders? Probably the fact that this topic, the
subject of countless leadership books on the market, is at once
inspiring and daunting. Inspiring, because as Scriptures state,
without a vision (or goals) "the people perish"; daunting,
because once you set a high-water mark as your destination,
you have to accomplish it. The good news is that the very act
of setting goals—and especially of writing them down—opens
up the possibility of achieving them. Stated succinctly, goal
setting itself must be the continual goal of a leader, because

that perpetual reaching for the brass ring—going for lofty goals of worth—will keep your organization vital and your leadership strong.

Grady gave lip-service to the practice of setting goals in his bagel shop, but when he started taking goals seriously, he got serious results. If you had asked him a year ago what his business goals were, he would have told you "to be the top bagel-seller in my community." That in itself was no small task, because a well-known chain bagel shop sat just a few miles down the road, attracting a steady stream of customers. However, Grady knew (and several loyal customers happily agreed) that his bagels were better. His dough was made fresh on the premises, not shipped in frozen packages. Plus, he wielded his father's secret bagel recipe from his days as a New York bagel-maker.

Although Grady held his own against the chain for a year, he decided head-to-head wasn't good enough. He sat down one night and wrote out a goal statement. Instead of selling x number of bagels in the coming year, he wanted to sell x-times-3. He posted that goal statement over his computer and reminded himself of it every time he drove by the chain bagel shop and saw the many cars parked outside. He encouraged his counter staff to memorize the goal too. Each time they had a banner sales day, surpassing a predetermined number of bagels sold, the staff earned a gift certificate to a favorite restaurant.

As the weeks and months went by, a change slowly started to take place. Invigorated by the written goal, the staff made selling bagels into a fun contest of sorts. Word of mouth spread about Grady's bagels, and the sales racked up. At year-end, Grady realized he had not only met his goal but surpassed it. All because he set a concrete goal, kept it in view, and steered straight for the horizon.

The apostle Paul wrote about goals in his letter to the Philippian believers, urging them to follow his example by "forgetting those things which are behind and reaching forward to those things which are ahead" (Philippians 3:13 NKJV). Though Paul's words address spiritual goals, his key point is relevant to all goals: You must leave the past behind if you want to reach for the future. Let go of disappointments and unrealized dreams to create new goals worth striving for. Ask God to give you direction as you chart a course of action, and consult Him along the way to make sure your progress remains true to His purpose for your life.

Like Grady, why not take the time to set down in writing one or two things you'd like to accomplish—in the next week(s), month(s), or year(s)? There's no prescribed length of time for goal setting; only that which you deem goal-worthy. Network with other leaders and find out what types of goals they set. Pick their brains about how they go about meeting those goals. At the same time, you want to tailor your goals to your specific organization's needs, and keep in mind that one leader's highest goal may be another's past accomplishment. No matter. What's important is that the goal be challenging enough to stretch you yet reasonable enough to be attained. At the same time, it's been said you should set out to accomplish something so big that without God's help you're bound to fail. As you keep goal setting, you'll keep growing.

I Will

Consult God before making any plans for my life. _____ yes _____ no

Watch for signs that indicate I'm heading in the right direction. _____ yes _____ no

Remember that only God knows the future. _____ yes _____ no

Be open to whatever plot twists God has in store for me. _____ yes _____ no

Live in the present but keep looking toward the future. _____ yes _____ no

Make vision casting a regular part of my life. _____ yes _____ no

Reach for the brass ring in every area of my life. _____ yes _____ no

Things to Do

- [ ] *Prepare a one-sentence vision statement for your organization, and post it where everyone can read it.*

- [ ] *Decide what you can do today that fits in with God's plan for your life.*

- [ ] *Write out five short-term and five long-term goals for your organization.*

- [ ] *Set a date on your planner each month for checking your progress on the goals you wrote.*

- [ ] *Stretch yourself to include one "impossible" dream in your list of life goals, and check your progress yearly.*

- [ ] *Why should anyone reveal personal goals to their boss? Research goal setting on the Internet (http://www.nwlink.com/~donclark/leader/leadled.html) and apply at least one principle this week.*

Things to Remember

Henceforth there is laid up for me a crown of righteousness, which the Lord, the righteous judge, shall give me at that day: and not to me only, but unto all them also that love his appearing.

2 TIMOTHY 4:8 KJV

Do you not know that those who run in a race all run, but one receives the prize? Run in such a way that you may obtain it.

1 CORINTHIANS 9:24 NKJV

I can do everything God asks me to with the help of Christ who gives me the strength and power.
Philippians 4:13 TLB

Delight yourself in the LORD; and He will give you the desires of your heart.

PSALM 37:4 NASB

He shall be like a tree planted by the rivers of water, that brings forth its fruit in its season, whose leaf also shall not wither; and whatever he does shall prosper.

PSALM 1:3 NKJV

God's Spirit beckons. There are things to do and places to go!

ROMANS 8:14 THE MESSAGE

Whatever you do, work at it with all your heart, as working for the Lord, not for men, since you know that you will receive an inheritance from the Lord as a reward. It is the Lord Christ you are serving.

COLOSSIANS 3:23–24 NIV

Let the beauty of the LORD our God be upon us: and establish thou the work of our hands upon us; yea, the work of our hands establish thou it.

PSALM 90:17 KJV

You are receiving the goal of your faith—the salvation of your souls.

1 PETER 1:9 NCV

Gray hair is a crown of splendor; it is attained by a righteous life.

PROVERBS 16:31 NIV

Godly people find life; evil people find death.

PROVERBS 11:19 NLT

There is surely a future hope for you, and your hope will not be cut off.

PROVERBS 23:18 NIV

If you make the unconditional commitment to reach your most important goals, if the strength of your decision is sufficient, you will find the way and the power to achieve your goals.

—ROBERT CONKLIN

No matter how carefully you plan your goals they will never be more than pipe dreams unless you pursue them with gusto.

—W. CLEMENT STONE

Finding Balance

The Great Leveler

[Paul wrote:] The very God of peace sanctify you wholly; and I pray God your whole spirit and soul and body be preserved blameless unto the coming of our Lord Jesus Christ.

—1 THESSALONIANS 5:23 KJV

How's your balance these days? Not your ability to walk without falling, but your knack for giving equal attention to your body, mind, and spirit. It's a rare person who has all three aspects of their being in perfect balance, and it's an even rarer person who knows how to measure the attention they give to each aspect. Even though you may not be able to determine when your life is perfectly balanced, you can always tell when it's imbalanced.

For people like you who shoulder a tremendous amount of responsibility, that imbalance is likely to be focused in the mind. Your mind works overtime as you puzzle out solutions to problems, clarify your hopes and dreams and projections for the future, and consider the pressing needs of those you lead. It may be difficult to remember the last time you took a mental break; even as you tried to relax on the beach during your last vacation, your thoughts regularly returned to the work you left behind and the agenda awaiting you on your return.

If you don't change that scenario soon, your neglect of your physical, emotional, and spiritual needs will take its toll on you and throw your life out of whack. Making the necessary changes, of course, is easier said than done, especially when you are carrying what feels like a truckload of burdens. But it can be done.

Start by asking yourself what advice you would give to people in your organization whose lives were clearly imbalanced, particularly those who place greater emphasis on the "mind" aspect of their lives (if that is your area of imbalance). You would probably suggest making small, incremental changes: Get out and take a walk every day, do some aerobics at home, and later join a gym if you feel you would use it. Do something simply for the sheer joy it brings to your life; become so immersed in a hobby or another fun activity that you forget all about work. Spend five minutes a day with God, then ten, then fifteen; take a one-hour spiritual retreat this weekend and work your way toward an entire day-long retreat.

Then follow your own advice. Many leaders find it easy to figure out what it takes to improve people's lives, but when it comes to their own, they exempt themselves from all those excellent suggestions they give other people! Don't be that kind of leader. Bless yourself the way you bless others, and allow God to bless you in even greater measure.

I Will

Take care of my body, mind, and spirit. _yes_ _no_

Be aware of the indications that my life has become unbalanced. _yes_ _no_

Allow God to bless me with a balanced life. _yes_ _no_

Realize that I can enjoy life even as I am fulfilling the mission I believe God has given me. _yes_ _no_

Understand that my performance as a leader will be enhanced by the attention I give to my body and spirit as well as to my mind. _yes_ _no_

Learn to relax. _yes_ _no_

Things to Do

☐ On a scale of one to five, rate the level of attention you give to each of the three aspects of your life, with one being little or no attention.

☐ Try a type of physical exercise you've never attempted before but think you might enjoy.

☐ List three activities that you would love to do if you only had the time. Then make the time and do them.

☐ Nurture your spirit by finding a devotional book that you could read a little of each day, like John C. Maxwell's Leadership Promises for Every Day.

☐ Spend ten to fifteen minutes meditating on God's love for you, bringing your mind back to His love whenever a distracting thought enters it.

☐ Memorize a psalm that has special meaning for you; try Psalm 1 or Psalm 15 for starters.

Things to Remember

Let all things be done decently
and in order.

1 CORINTHIANS 14:40 NKJV

[Paul wrote:] Though I am absent in the
flesh, yet I am with you in spirit,
rejoicing to see your good order and the
steadfastness of your faith in Christ.

COLOSSIANS 2:5 NKJV

[Jesus said:] "Take care to live in me, and
let me live in you. For a branch can't
produce fruit when severed from the
vine. Nor can you be fruitful apart
from me."

JOHN 15:4 TLB

Jesus answered and said to her, "Martha,
Martha, you are worried and troubled
about many things. But one thing is
needed, and Mary has chosen that good
part, which will not be taken away
from her."

LUKE 10:41–42 NKJV

Let your moderation be known unto all
men. The Lord is at hand.

PHILIPPIANS 4:5 KJV

[Paul wrote:] I don't mean that others
should have relief while you have
hardship. Rather, it's a matter of striking
a balance.

2 CORINTHIANS 8:13
GOD'S WORD

In a balanced
organization,
working towards a
common objective,
there is success.

—T. L. SCRUTTON

Just as your car
runs more smoothly
and requires less
energy to go faster
and farther when
the wheels are in
perfect alignment,
you perform better
when your
thoughts, feelings,
emotions, goals,
and values are in
balance.

—BRIAN TRACY

Competition

Being Your Best

Be devoted to one another in brotherly love. Honor one another above yourselves.

—ROMANS 12:10 NIV

When Betty opened a bookshop and café in the restored district of downtown, customers flocked to sample her store's cozy combination of steaming java and front list titles. It was the kind of place where book lovers were encouraged to browse and linger. Every time the bell over the door jingled, Betty happily envisioned a potential sale at the cash register. That all changed the day a huge bookseller chain moved in a few blocks down the street. They had a café too—and thousands more titles than Betty could ever hope to stock. Suddenly, the joy went out of bookselling for her. As she watched her steady stream of customers dwindle to a trickle, her brimming goodwill threatened to turn to bitterness.

Competition: It's a word business owners know like their own middle names—and one they often live in quiet dread of. Yet, ironically, many business leaders have learned to approach competition as a blessing in disguise. The true-grit determination that makes a free enterprise system so effective raises the bar for everyone—rendering products and services in a constant state of improvement. Those in business often find that competition not only keeps them on their toes, it brings out their creative and productive best.

Refusing to be vanquished, Betty decided to play up her strengths—those aspects of indie ownership that a chain would struggle to match, like overwhelming customer service, adding the personal touch to every sale, and making her store a home for the reading community. Over the ensuing months, she and her staff worked hard for their customers and surprised themselves by coming up with creative perks, such as poetry readings, open-mike nights that created a forum for artists and musicians, a staff's-picks recommended reading list, book clubs that linked with local schools for publicity and support, a finish-the-mystery writing contest for aspiring authors, and other programs. When Betty spotted one of the managers from the chain bookstore in her shop one day, she realized he was trolling for ideas—obviously curious about what *she* was doing right. Instead of resenting his presence, she introduced herself, complimenting the man on the success of his store and forming an unlikely friendship in the process.

It's easy to spout a biblical injunction to "honor one another above yourselves" but quite another matter to live it out in the world of business and the leadership world. Yet the resolve to live by high standards still issues a clarion call to anyone whose heart leans toward rightness.

Competition can bring out the best and worst in a leader. Make best behavior the order of your day. You'll never regret it.

I Will

Realize that competitors bring out the best in me. _yes_ _no_

Put my highest effort into my business or leadership endeavor. _yes_ _no_

Believe that God intends to work everything out for good as I put Him first in my life. _yes_ _no_

Be thankful for the chance to compete in the marketplace of ideas or products/services. _yes_ _no_

Understand that I am more than the bottom line. _yes_ _no_

Remember that those who strive to be first in the kingdom will end up last. _yes_ _no_

Things to Do

☐ *Choose someone you view as a rival, and pray for God's blessing on their business.*

☐ *Pray for God's blessing on your own business or leadership endeavor.*

☐ *Look for ways to add value to your products or services.*

☐ *Select one of the quotations on the facing page and tape it to your computer monitor.*

☐ *Consult your staff for ideas on how to be your competitive best as an organization.*

☐ *Think of a time when your organization's performance flagged and how you would act differently now.*

Things to Remember

Everyone who competes for the prize is temperate in all things. Now they do it to obtain a perishable crown, but we for an imperishable crown.

1 CORINTHIANS 9:25 NKJV

Similarly, if anyone competes as an athlete, he does not receive the victor's crown unless he competes according to the rules.

2 TIMOTHY 2:5 NIV

You will understand what is right, just, and fair, and you will know how to find the right course of action every time.

PROVERBS 2:9 NLT

The Rock: His works are perfect, and the way he works is fair and just; A God you can depend upon, no exceptions, a straight-arrow God.

DEUTERONOMY 32:4 THE MESSAGE

If someone wants to sue you and take your tunic, let him have your cloak as well. If someone forces you to go one mile, go with him two miles.

MATTHEW 5:40–41 NIV

If your enemies are hungry, feed them. If they are thirsty, give them something to drink, and they will be ashamed of what they have done to you.

ROMANS 12:20 NLT

Goodwill is the one and only asset that competition cannot undersell or destroy.

—MARSHALL FIELD

Thank God for competition. When our competitors upset our plans or outdo our designs, they open infinite possibilities of our own work to us.

—GIL ATKINSON

Generosity

A Leader Who Gives

[Jesus said:] "Give, and it will be given to you: good measure, pressed down, shaken together, and running over will be put into your bosom. For with the same measure that you use, it will be measured back to you."

—LUKE 6:38 NKJV

Though not its primary theme, Charles Dickens's classic tale *A Christmas Carol* contrasts two very different types of businessmen in the characters of Ebenezer Scrooge and Old Fezziwig, the man Scrooge is apprenticed to as a young man. In a vivid flashback scene conveyed by the Ghost of Christmas Past, Scrooge sees his young self preparing to make merry with Fezziwig, Fezziwig's family, and the other employees on Christmas Eve. They scurry to clear away the accounting books as a fiddler strikes up a lively tune and everyone grabs a dance partner. The older Scrooge, looking on, mutters to the ghost that Fezziwig was a fool, squandering his valuable time and money on merrymaking and a sumptuous feast when he ought to have poured it back into the company. Yet the compelling scene before him touches a deep place in his heart, and he begs the ghost to take him away from there. His old boss's generous nature goads his conscience.

The present-tense Scrooge, captured in all his bleak and lonely misery in the opening scene, is a wealthy man who scrimps on coal to save a few coins (and keeps his counting house uncomfortably cold because of it), doles out a meager wage to his employee Bob Cratchitt, and resents the fact that he'll have to pay Bob a day's wage on Christmas. Though rich in material things, Scrooge withholds generosity in the most crucial currency of all—that of goodwill to mankind. His miserly nature is never so cruel as when he scrimps on kindness toward his fellow human beings.

Fezziwig, on the other hand, pays his employees fairly and, more important, invests himself in them as individuals. Readers get the impression he spreads joy and generosity of spirit wherever he goes, and everyone he comes in contact with is the richer for it.

Unlike Scrooge, you won't get the opportunity to see how people react when you die, or read the words written on your tombstone. But his ghostly wake-up call serves as a reminder. What *would* your employees say about you if you were suddenly gone tomorrow? Would they recall a kind, generous leader who gave in "good measure, pressed down, shaken together, and running over"? Or would they whisper with relief that you were finally out of the way?

When Jesus talked about generosity He referred to more than financial matters. That's because giving springs from a generous heart and reaches into all areas of life. The giving leader not only pays fair wages but also gives of himself. The generous leader is willing to give others a chance to shine, rather than hoarding all the glory for himself. It's been said that the difference between a selfish and a giving leader is this: When the selfish leader's company achieves a goal, he looks in the mirror and says, "Look what I did," while the generous leader says, "Look what we did" (emphasizing teamwork). Conversely, when the company takes a hit, the selfish leader blames his staff while the generous leader takes responsibility for the failure.

At the same time, generosity should not be confused with careless liberality. No one profits from the leader who is so lax in his dealings that the organization suffers. Even Jesus, who personified generosity while He walked the earth, was a leader of common sense. He recognized the need for material provision, yet trusted His Father to provide for it. When one of His followers asked whether it was lawful to pay taxes, Jesus replied, "Render therefore to Caesar the things that are Caesar's, and to God the things that are God's" (Matthew 22:21 NKJV). In other words, keep fairness as the uppermost law in all your business dealings, and God will see to it that your needs are met.

While it's true some people are born with a generous nature, generosity is the mark of maturity. It's also the flipside of thankfulness. As you look around at those you lead today, make a mental list of their best qualities and allow yourself to bask in thankfulness for those traits. The very act of being thankful will stimulate a generous response in you, and, like Fezziwig, you'll find those around you made richer for it. Along with the ghost of Jacob Marley, you will be able to say, "Business? Mankind was my business."

I Will

Change my attitude from one of having to give to
one of being able to give.   yes   no
                                                             ____   ____

Define my love for others by my willingness to give
up things I value for their sake.   yes   no
                                                             ____   ____

Make generosity a life mission.   yes   no
                                                             ____   ____

Thank God for all He's given me.   yes   no
                                                             ____   ____

Develop a heart attitude of perpetual giving.   yes   no
                                                             ____   ____

Train myself to think in terms of more than money
when I hear the word *generosity*.   yes   no
                                                             ____   ____

Things to Do

☐ *Look for opportunities to be a behind-the-scenes giver.*

☐ *List five ways, other than money, through which you can be
generous to others.*

☐ *Practice random acts of kindness and generosity.*

☐ *Offer to go the extra mile for someone, especially when you
don't have to.*

☐ *Model servant leadership in your organization.*

☐ *Write a real-world definition of what Luke 6:38 means to you.*

☐ *Verbalize thanks for generosity you spot in others.*

Things to Remember

My God shall supply all your need according to His riches in glory by Christ Jesus.

PHILIPPIANS 4:19 NKJV

His master replied, "Well done, good and faithful servant! You have been faithful with a few things; I will put you in charge of many things. Come and share your master's happiness!"

MATTHEW 25:23 NIV

A generous man will himself be blessed, for he shares his food with the poor.
Proverbs 22:9 NIV

Good people leave their wealth to their grandchildren, but a sinner's wealth is stored up for good people.

PROVERBS 13:22 NCV

You are enriched in everything for all liberality, which causes thanksgiving through us to God.

2 CORINTHIANS 9:11 NKJV

God so loved the world, that he gave his only begotten Son, that whosoever believeth in him should not perish, but have everlasting life.

JOHN 3:16 KJV

Don't forget to help others and to share your possessions with them. This too is like offering a sacrifice that pleases God.

HEBREWS 13:16 CEV

Let each one give as he purposes in his heart, not grudgingly or of necessity; for God loves a cheerful giver.

2 CORINTHIANS 9:7 NKJV

Giving a gift works wonders; it may bring you before important people!

PROVERBS 18:16 NLT

It is possible to give away and become richer! It is also possible to hold on too tightly and lose everything.

PROVERBS 11:24 TLB

Tell them to use their money to do good. They should be rich in good works and should give generously to those in need, always being ready to share with others whatever God has given them.

1 TIMOTHY 6:18 NLT

When you are harvesting in your field and you overlook a sheaf, do not go back to get it. Leave it for the alien, the fatherless and the widow, so that the LORD your God may bless you in all the work of your hands.

DEUTERONOMY 24:19 NIV

I take as my guide the hope of a saint: in crucial things, unity . . . in important things, diversity . . . in all things, generosity.

—GEORGE BUSH

He who gives what he would as readily throw away, gives without generosity; for the essence of generosity is in self sacrifice.

—SIR HENRY TAYLOR

Respect

Give It to Get It

[David wrote:] Lord, you are my shield, my glory, and my only hope. You alone can lift my head, now bowed in shame.

—PSALM 3:3 TLB

Fresh out of seminary, Jeffrey was offered a position as youth pastor at a suburban church. He knew deep down that he had a difficult time relating to younger teens in particular. But with college loans to repay and only one job offer, he felt he didn't have much of a choice—especially once his prayer buddies weighed in with a unanimous thumbs-up.

When things got off to a rocky start, though, Jeffrey shrugged it off, figuring that he and the middle-schoolers just needed some time to adjust to each other. In truth, what Jeffrey really wanted was for the youth to adjust to *him*; he believed he knew what was best for them. After all, he reasoned, it was his job to keep them in line, so he simply needed to exert a bit more control. Within six months, though, Jeffrey was ready to call it quits. Before he could, the senior pastor received a laundry list of parents' complaints about the youth leadership and decided to intervene, calling Jeffrey in to discuss the problems in his ministry.

"The kids just don't have any respect for my authority,"

Jeffrey complained. "I realize I'm not that much older than they are, but still . . ." As his voice trailed off, the pastor began to gently show him how his lack of respect for the youth had cost him their respect. His failure to genuinely listen, his inability to trust, and his disregard for their suggestions had caused those he was attempting to lead to ultimately reject his leadership.

Jeffrey was fortunate to learn the number one lesson about respect early in his career: In order to gain respect from others, you must extend respect to others. He had failed to see how his followers were interpreting his actions. Furthermore, he had failed to realize that respect is not a perk that comes automatically with a particular title or position; respect is an honor that must be earned over time.

Earning respect is as simple as following the Golden Rule—treating other people the way you want them to treat you. Think back to the various authority figures and leaders who have influenced your life. Those that you have the most respect for are most likely those who treated you with respect, regardless of your age or position or status in relation to theirs.

Be an example of respectful behavior for your followers. Encourage them to respect each other as well as you and anyone else in authority over them. And remember—anything less than earned respect is no respect at all.

I Will

Treat my followers in the way I want to be treated. ___yes___ ___no___

Realize that I must earn respect. ___yes___ ___no___

Encourage those in my organization to treat each other with respect. ___yes___ ___no___

Be aware that my followers may not interpret my actions in the way I intended them to. ___yes___ ___no___

Respect the people I lead regardless of their age, position, or status. ___yes___ ___no___

Show my respect by listening and taking suggestions seriously. ___yes___ ___no___

Things to Do

☐ Read the short New Testament book of Philemon, which could serve as a case study in showing respect for authority.

☐ List the things you think your followers should do to show their respect for you—and see if you have acted in similar ways toward them.

☐ Think back to leaders you have respected and write about the ways they showed respect for you.

☐ Develop a code of respect—a list of guidelines for showing high regard and esteem toward others—for your organization. Sign it and pledge to follow it yourself.

☐ Reflect on John W. Gardner's quotation and consider how it applies to your role as a leader.

☐ Show your respect for those in authority over you by adding their names to your prayer list.

Things to Remember

Sanctify Christ as Lord in your hearts, always being ready to make a defense to everyone who asks you to give an account for the hope that is in you, yet with gentleness and reverence.

1 PETER 3:15 NASB

All slaves who believe must give complete respect to their own masters. In this way no one will speak evil of God's name and what we teach.

1 TIMOTHY 6:1 GOD'S WORD

Be responsive to your pastoral leaders. Listen to their counsel. They are alert to the condition of your lives and work under the strict supervision of God. Contribute to the joy of their leadership, not its drudgery. Why would you want to make things harder for them?

HEBREWS 13:17 THE MESSAGE

The kings and queens of those nations where they were raised will come and bow down. They will take care of you just like a slave taking care of a child. Then you will know that I am the LORD. You won't be disappointed if you trust me.

ISAIAH 49:23 CEV

Do not exalt yourself in the king's presence, and do not claim a place among great men.

PROVERBS 25:6 NIV

There is no respect for others without humility in one's self.

—HENRI FREDERIC AMIEL

If you have some respect for people as they are, you can be more effective in helping them to become better than they are.

—JOHN W. GARDNER

Enjoyment

Time for Play

[Jesus said:] "A thief comes only to rob, kill, and destroy.
I came so that everyone would have life, and have it in its
fullest."

—John 10:10 CEV

When Gavin and Jenni assumed leadership of the couples'
fellowship at their church, they were glad to have the
opportunity to share with other couples all God had shown
them about building strong relationships. For weeks, they
pored over the Scriptures and countless books on marriage as
they designed a curriculum customized for the couples in their
group.

They looked forward to the weekly meetings and
considered themselves blessed to be a part of a group that gave
so much more than they took. Soon they began to make plans
for a couples' retreat, a project that seemed to consume most
of their waking hours. But they knew it was worth it.

Things changed, though, when they returned home from
the event. "Honey," Gavin said to his wife, "do you realize we
spent the whole weekend working on the 'next session' while
all the other couples were enjoying the retreat?" Jenni agreed.
Although the couples' group had enriched their lives, she said,
they had taken their responsibility so seriously that they had

forgotten to have fun—something they had encouraged other couples to never forget.

Gavin and Jenni caught the tendency to take their responsibility too seriously before any harm was done. But others in leadership have not been so fortunate. They've suffered from health problems and damaged relationships, among other difficulties, all because they failed to take the time to enjoy the life God gave them.

You're probably well aware of how important recreation is. Like Gavin and Jenni, you have probably even emphasized that to the people you lead. But when it comes to finding the time to have some fun for yourself, you can't seem to fit it in to your already overloaded schedule. You promise yourself that after the next project is completed or once the next event is over, you'll go out and play.

If you've been putting off taking time for yourself, the time to go out and play is now. You're long overdue. The benefits will outweigh any challenges that you will face if you drop everything just to have some fun. Not only will you benefit personally by feeling refreshed and rejuvenated, but also your organization will benefit by having a leader who is refreshed and rejuvenated.

I Will

Learn to play again.   yes ___ no ___

Encourage people in my organization to take
time for enjoyment.   yes ___ no ___

Realize the consequences of failing to take time
for myself.   yes ___ no ___

Stop taking my responsibilities too seriously.   yes ___ no ___

Plan for regular leisure activities.   yes ___ no ___

Understand that God wants me to enjoy my life
with Him.   yes ___ no ___

Be thankful for the opportunities I have to be
refreshed and rejuvenated.   yes ___ no ___

Things to Do

☐ Plan a "play day" for your organization, a time when everyone can get
together just to have fun.

☐ List the things you enjoy but seldom take time to do, and schedule
three of those activities in the next three weeks.

☐ Make plans with your spouse or a friend for a weekend getaway—and
leave the laptop home.

☐ Meet with others in your organization to decide on ways to celebrate
the completion of a project or a similar milestone.

☐ Make a pact with another leader to keep each other accountable to
take the time off when you need to.

☐ Read through the Gospel of Mark, noting all the times Jesus either took
time for Himself or spent time simply enjoying life with others.

Things to Remember

[Jesus said:] "I, the Son of Man, feast and drink, and you say, 'He's a glutton and a drunkard, and a friend of the worst sort of sinners!' But wisdom is shown to be right by what results from it."

MATTHEW 11:19 NLT

A cheerful look brings joy to the heart, and good news gives health to the bones.

PROVERBS 15:30 NIV

This is the day the LORD has made; let us rejoice and be glad in it.

PSALM 118:24 NIV

Then our mouth was filled with laughter and our tongue with joyful shouting; then they said among the nations, "The LORD has done great things for them."

PSALM 126:2 NASB

[David wrote:] You will show me the path of life; in Your presence is fullness of joy; at Your right hand are pleasures forevermore.

PSALM 16:11 NKJV

Find out for yourself how good the LORD is. Happy are those who find safety with him.

PSALM 34:8 GNT

Enjoy the journey, enjoy every moment, and quit worrying about winning and losing.

—MATT BIONDI

It is essential to our well-being, and to our lives, that we play and enjoy life. Every single day do something that makes your heart sing.

—MARCIA WIEDER

Communication

Word Wise

Let your conversation be always full of grace, seasoned with salt, so that you may know how to answer everyone.

—COLOSSIANS 4:6 NIV

As the CEO of a leading communications company, Allen prided himself on the high degree of interaction between the senior executives and the rest of the staff. Daily e-mails apprised employees of new developments in the company or milestones among the staff, such as birthdays, while weekly electronic newsletters updated everyone on the status of major projects.

A monthly print newsletter—nearly a relic in the industry—allowed executives to provide more detailed information and included lots of little tidbits designed to motivate the staff and give them ideas for working more efficiently. But Allen's confidence in his company's ability to communicate effectively was shattered as he scanned the results of an on-line survey sent to every employee. The survey sought input on the staff's assessment of the major challenges facing the corporation.

To Allen's surprise, "communication" was far and away the most frequently mentioned problem in the communications company. Puzzled, Allen discussed the situation with several colleagues, one of whom suggested offering employees an opportunity to anonymously elaborate on the problem as they saw it. Although responses varied, nearly everyone identified lack of communication *from* employees as a reason for their discontent. Many offered specific and practical advice on how to correct the situation.

Management immediately implemented some of their suggestions, starting with providing employees with a means of offering helpful feedback on company decisions, without fear of repercussions. Executives and managers became more responsive to e-mails from employees, treating their requests with the same timeliness, courtesy, and importance they would extend to customers' requests. And once a month, the company held what came to jokingly be known as a "free-for-all"—not a wild melee but a meeting in which employees were free to speak their minds in an open forum.

Allen learned a crucial lesson from the survey responses and the resulting improvement in communication: True communication only occurs when each party in the "conversation" has a voice. His original effort to stay in touch with his employees was admirable, but it met only half of their communication needs.

A great deal of your value as a leader rests on your ability to clearly convey information to others and accurately receive information from others. You'll know you have acquired that ability when your communication results in a sense that the people involved genuinely connected with each other.

Becoming a good communicator simply involves mastering certain skills and some focus on what's going on inside your head when you're speaking with someone: Think before you speak. Resist distraction. Maintain eye contact.

Concentrate both on what you're saying and what you're hearing. Avoid crafting a mental response before the other person is finished talking.

Then there are numerous pointers relating to speaking before a group: Keep it short. Use concrete rather than abstract terms. Make your speech memorable by telling stories and anecdotes that get your point across. Provide an opportunity for questions and answers, written feedback, or an informal session with the audience after your talk.

Acquiring the necessary skills to become a better communicator need not be expensive or time consuming; there's an abundance of books, courses, Web sites and organizations dedicated to better communication. Even better, you have access to God, who spoke the world into existence and initiated a two-way conversation with His people.

Finally, you have the example of Jesus, who not only spoke the truth to His followers but also listened to what they had to say. He engaged people in dialogue, frequently asking them questions instead of monopolizing the conversation. Everywhere He went, He made a connection with others through the words He spoke—and the way He spoke. He was clearly accessible and approachable, the kind of leader people could talk with in an easy and familiar manner.

Keep that word *connection* in mind as you communicate with others. Let people know that they can talk things over with you. Make sure you provide an opportunity for other voices to be heard. Learn from Jesus and rely on God to help you use words to make a solid connection with your team.

I Will

Strive to become a better communicator.

yes   *no*

Learn the art of conversation from the example
of Jesus.

yes   *no*

Give everyone a chance to be heard.

yes   *no*

Encourage honest and open feedback in my
organization.

yes   *no*

Understand the importance of connecting with my
audience.

yes   *no*

Ask God to show me how I can improve my ability to
communicate.

yes   *no*

Things to Do

☐ *Look into joining Toastmasters (www.toastmasters.org) or another organization that has a proven history of helping people communicate more effectively.*

☐ *Immediately implement a method, or a better method, of generating feedback from the people you lead.*

☐ *Schedule a "free-for-all" meeting in which the people in your organization are free to courteously speak their minds without fear of repercussion.*

☐ *Create a procedure for following up on suggestions or complaints you receive from the people you lead.*

☐ *Highlight the concrete, visual words and phrases in your last speech or article; the less highlighting, the more you need to improve next time.*

☐ *Ask a colleague you trust to assess your communication skills and offer tips on how you could do better.*

Things to Remember

Put these things out of your life: anger, bad temper, doing or saying things to hurt others, and using evil words when you talk.

COLOSSIANS 3:8 NCV

Let no corrupt word proceed out of your mouth, but what is good for necessary edification, that it may impart grace to the hearers.

EPHESIANS 4:29 NKJV

*Use sound words that cannot be criticized,
so that your enemies may be put to shame
by not having anything bad to say about us.*
Titus 2:8 GNT

Let him who is taught the word share in all good things with him who teaches.

GALATIANS 6:6 NKJV

Have you been caught by your own words, trapped by your own promises?

PROVERBS 6:2 GNT

They [the wicked] wink and make gestures to deceive you.

PROVERBS 6:13 GNT

[David wrote:] I have proclaimed the good news of righteousness in the great assembly; indeed, I do not restrain my lips, O LORD, You Yourself know.

PSALM 40:9 NKJV

Christ is the one through whom God created everything in heaven and earth. He made the things we can see and the things we can't see—kings, kingdoms, rulers, and authorities. Everything has been created through him and for him.

COLOSSIANS 1:16 NLT

Jesus answered by quoting Deuteronomy: "It takes more than bread to stay alive. It takes a steady stream of words from God's mouth."

MATTHEW 4:4 THE MESSAGE

[Jesus said:] "You only make things worse when you lay down a smoke screen of pious talk, saying, 'I'll pray for you,' and never doing it, or saying, 'God be with you,' and not meaning it. You don't make your words true by embellishing them with religious lace. In making your speech sound more religious, it becomes less true."

MATTHEW 5:34 THE MESSAGE

[Jesus said:] "Just say 'yes' and 'no.' When you manipulate words to get your own way, you go wrong."

MATTHEW 5:37 THE MESSAGE

[Jesus said:] "The Spirit of your Father will supply the words."

MATTHEW 10:20 THE MESSAGE

The art of communication is the language of leadership.

—JAMES HUMES

Your ability to communicate is an important tool in your pursuit of your goals, whether it is with your family, your coworkers or your clients and customers.

—LES BROWN

Strength

What Is Your Strong Suit?

[David wrote:] When I pray, you answer me; you encourage me by giving me the strength I need.

—Psalm 138:3 NLT

Leaders attribute their strength to any number of sources—their upbringing and family life, a network of supporters who keep them going, a loving spouse, an outstanding mentor and role model.

But there are other sources of strength that are far more powerful and have a far more lasting effect—namely God and His Word. When you draw strength from His Spirit and the Bible, you tap into a source of energy that will last through eternity. Couple that with your own inner resolve, and you have what it takes to keep you going . . . and going.

Maintaining the strength you need to continue to be effective as a leader requires a fair amount of exercise—not the kind you do at a fitness center but the kind you can do wherever you are. Keeping spiritually fit is the key, and that involves an intimate relationship with God, one that you nurture and protect at all costs. That relationship needs to be the top priority in your life, because your fitness in every other area of your life—your work, your relationships, your community of faith—depends on the quality of your fellowship with God.

Drawing on God's strength requires trusting Him completely, which is something of a paradox. But the Bible says that God's way of doing things is often very different from the way people think things should be done. Instead of trying to muster the strength you need all on your own, you can turn to Him in prayer and ask Him to replace your weakness with His strength. Admitting your weakness and relying on Him actually makes you stronger.

David and the other psalmists understood that paradox well. In praying to God and praising Him, they found the strength to face their enemies—and their own weaknesses—and overcome them. The book of Psalms is a testament to the strength God gives His people and a good place to start reading if you feel you need a bit more spiritual muscle.

Most people sense their strength failing them at times; it's part of being human. Whenever you feel that happening to you, whenever you detect a weakness in your role as a leader or in your everyday life, ask God to give you the strength you need. Learn to see your weaknesses not as a liability but as a reminder that God wants you to turn to Him in complete dependence.

I Will

Recognize God as the source of my strength.   _____ yes   _____ no

Flex my spiritual muscle by maintaining my
relationship with God.   _____ yes   _____ no

Depend on God completely.   _____ yes   _____ no

Admit my weaknesses.   _____ yes   _____ no

Recognize the toll the demands of leadership
can take.   _____ yes   _____ no

Turn to God before I begin to feel drained.   _____ yes   _____ no

Maintain fitness in every area of my life.   _____ yes   _____ no

Things to Do

☐ *Using a concordance, read every verse in Psalms that refers to the strength God gives His people.*

☐ *Develop a spiritual fitness program incorporating prayer, Bible reading, and Bible study.*

☐ *List your weaknesses and ask God to give you strength in those areas.*

☐ *Read the story of Samson—considered the strongest man in the region at the time—in Judges 14–16.*

☐ *Make a list of the people who have helped you to become, and stay, strong. Thank as many as you can.*

☐ *Read* Leadership *by former New York Mayor Rudy Giuliani, whose strength affected millions in the aftermath of September 11.*

Things to Remember

[Jesus said:] " 'You shall love the LORD your God with all your heart, with all your soul, with all your mind, and with all your strength.' This is the first commandment."

MARK 12:30 NKJV

Nehemiah told the people, "Enjoy your good food and wine and share some with those who didn't have anything to bring. Don't be sad! This is a special day for the LORD, and he will make you happy and strong."

NEHEMIAH 8:10 CEV

If you falter in times of trouble, how small is your strength!

PROVERBS 24:10 NIV

[David wrote:] He is the God who makes me strong, who makes my pathway safe.

PSALM 18:32 GNT

[The psalmist wrote:] God is our refuge and strength, an ever-present help in trouble.

PSALM 46:1 NIV

[Asaph wrote:] My flesh and my heart may fail, but God is the strength of my heart and my portion forever.

PSALM 73:26 NIV

Strength is a matter of a made up mind.

—JOHN BEECHER

Superior strength is found in the long run to lie with those who had right on their side.

—JAMES A. FROUDE

Delegating Authority

Many Hands, Light Work

[Jethro said to Moses:] "Both you and these people who are with you will surely wear yourselves out. For this thing is too much for you; you are not able to perform it by yourself."

—EXODUS 18:18 NKJV

When Samantha received her long-awaited promotion to manager, she was more than ready to demonstrate her abilities. This was her chance to shine, her opportunity to show what she was made of. In her zeal to make an impression, she hoarded duties for herself, abiding by the motto "If you want something done right, do it yourself." The problem was that there was only so much of herself to go around. One day after lunch a trusted mentor encouraged her to relinquish her grip on two or three pet projects and trust key people to get the job done. "It'll require trust on your part, but you'll set your people free," the mentor said. Sure enough, when she let go of the reins, those key staffers in turn stepped up to the plate and showed what they were made of. Samantha's workload is a lot more manageable these days.

Samantha discovered that something magical happens when people are expected to shine—and given the freedom to do so.

Offering up your best leadership skills day by day is what

defines you as a leader. It's what makes others want to follow you. That skill set is only complete when it includes a healthy ability to delegate to others.

Almost everyone knows what it's like to work for a leader who doesn't trust in his or her people. The resulting low morale grows so thick it is almost palpable. Contrast that to the organization that spreads enthusiasm and a you-can-do-it attitude down every hall.

Moses staggered under the weight of leading the Israelites who followed him into the wilderness toward the promised land. Like all competent leaders, he was simply trying to do the task assigned to him—in this case, by God. But his father-in-law, Jethro, saw a man in trouble and stepped in with some timely advice. Because Moses was open to Jethro's wisdom, the camp of Israel was divided into manageable groups, each with its own judge, or leader. God did not strip the leadership mantle from Moses—he was still the one ultimately responsible for the people—but the reduced burden allowed him to lead from strength rather than chronic exhaustion.

Entrust appropriate projects to the people you lead, and you all will win.

I Will

Remember that many hands really do make
light work.
yes _no_

Be aware that God ordained the principle of
delegating authority.
yes _no_

Cultivate trust in others on a daily basis.
yes _no_

Wear my heart—and my expectations—on
my sleeve.
yes _no_

Appreciate that delegating authority is not the
same thing as passing the buck.
yes _no_

Be thankful for the people God has placed under
my leadership.
yes _no_

Keep alert for opportunities to let others shine.
yes _no_

Things to Do

☐ *Think of three projects you can delegate to capable people.*

☐ *Let go of one pet project this week.*

☐ *Create opportunities for your staff to rise to the occasion, and give them positive feedback on their performance.*

☐ *Study the story of Moses and Jethro in Exodus 18 for an overview of why delegation is so important.*

☐ *Keep a chart of how many times those you lead "shine" this month.*

Things to Remember

Commit your works to the LORD, and your thoughts will be established.

PROVERBS 16:3 NKJV

Plans go wrong for lack of advice; many counselors bring success.

PROVERBS 15:22 NLT

[God] handed out gifts of apostle, prophet, evangelist, and pastor-teacher to train Christians in skilled servant work, working within Christ's body, the church.

EPHESIANS 4:11–12 THE MESSAGE

You shall select out of all the people able men who fear God, men of truth, those who hate dishonest gain; and you shall place these over them as leaders of thousands, of hundreds, of fifties and of tens.

EXODUS 18:21 NASB

Timothy, guard what has been entrusted to your care. Turn away from godless chatter and the opposing ideas of what is falsely called knowledge.

1 TIMOTHY 6:20 NIV

The king said to the servant, "Excellent! You are a good servant. Since I can trust you with small things, I will let you rule over ten of my cities."

LUKE 19:17 NCV

Delegating work works, provided the one delegating works, too.

—ROBERT HALF

Delegating means letting others become the experts and hence the best.

—TIMOTHY FIRNSTAHL

Humility

Humble Pie

Be content with who you are, and don't put on airs. God's strong hand is on you; he'll promote you at the right time.

—1 PETER 5:6 THE MESSAGE

Stop and reread that verse again. If believed wholeheartedly it will put an end to all your striving, all your worries, all your white-knuckling to succeed in leadership. After all, you can't get much better than a promise that God Himself—the One who holds the planets in place—"will promote you at the right time." The underlying intent of the apostle Peter's words is unvarnished humility. Be content, he says. Be humble. Don't try to be somebody you're not. Others won't be fooled anyway.

Of all the traits a godly leader can possess, humility ranks highest, for without a humble spirit no man or woman can fully be God's instrument. The only problem is that humility is often forged through difficulties—or, as the word implies, through times of humiliation. God's highest purpose for your life is that you be malleable clay on His potter's wheel. He intends to strip away your pride and mold you into the image of His Son. Only then will you be the leader He has called you to be.

Abraham Lincoln rose to political power during the United States' worst season of civil turmoil. As North raged against South, the human death toll climbed and the president's heart broke for the nation that seemed rent beyond repair. A naturally humble man, Lincoln looked to God for direction and national healing.

One of the most enduring images of Lincoln depicts him praying, head bowed, as he stands in the Oval Office. But it is his words that convey the true spirit of humility this leader possessed. As he dedicated the military cemetery at Gettysburg, he resolved that the dead should not have died in vain—"that this nation, under God, shall have a new birth of freedom."

Lincoln won reelection in 1864, and in his plans for peace he was generous and flexible, encouraging Southerners to lay down their arms and join the Union in mending the nation's wounds. That spirit of humility clearly guided him when he penned the words of his second inaugural address: "With malice toward none; with charity for all; with firmness in the right, as God gives us to see the right, let us strive on to finish the work we are in."

The apostle Peter had much to say about humility, and, given his history and temperament, he was in a good position to teach on the subject. Known for his arrogance and hot temper, Peter stands out among the twelve disciples as a brash instigator, a man accustomed to taking life by the horns and bending it to his will. But several chapters later, after he denied knowing Christ and then received forgiveness and a life mission from the risen Savior, a different man emerges from the pages of Scripture. The new Peter is still bold, but his boldness is tempered with humility and a profound understanding of God's grace. That's why he could write the words, "Clothe yourselves with humility toward one another, because, 'God opposes the proud but gives grace to the humble.' Humble yourselves, therefore, under God's mighty hand, that he may lift you up in due time" (1 Peter 5:5–6 NIV).

Another aspect to humility that The Message translation of 1 Peter 5:6 picks up on is contentment. Are you content in the role God has placed you in? Are you content with "who you are," as Peter so pointedly asks? True contentment springs from humility—a heart so set on God that it almost forgets about the self, placing God and others at the top of the priority list. If you struggle with contentment in your leadership role, ask God to give you the grace to be content. That's the kind of prayer He is quick to answer every time.

As you lead those whom God has placed under your care, keep your mind set on Him. By focusing on God, He in turn will keep you humble—and transform you into a leader worthy of shepherding others.

I Will

Develop a childlike trust in God and take His promise in 1 Peter 5 at face value.

yes _____ _no_ _____

Realize that humility is not the same thing as groveling.

yes _____ _no_ _____

Exchange brashness and arrogance for a heart set on God.

yes _____ _no_ _____

Think of others before myself.

yes _____ _no_ _____

Regard prayer as my first option, not my last, in situations that call for humility.

yes _____ _no_ _____

Be honest about my character flaws and ask God for a humble spirit.

yes _____ _no_ _____

Things to Do

☐ Read 1 Peter 5 and Luke 18 for insight into God's view of pride and humility.

☐ Make a list of the cost of keeping pride in your life.

☐ List several practical ways you can show humility toward those you lead.

☐ Read The Life You've Always Wanted by John Ortberg and ponder what the author means by "the discipline of humility."

☐ Go through the day with a put-others-first attitude.

☐ Inventory areas of pride in your life and submit them to God one by one.

Things to Remember

All of you be of one mind, having compassion for one another; love as brothers, be tenderhearted, be courteous.

1 PETER 3:8 NKJV

You save the humble but bring low those whose eyes are haughty.

PSALM 18:27 NIV

In Your majesty ride prosperously because of truth, humility, and righteousness; and Your right hand shall teach You awesome things.

PSALM 45:4 NKJV

Whoever exalts himself will be humbled, and he who humbles himself will be exalted.

Luke 14:11 NKJV

Who among you is wise and understanding? Let him show by his good behavior his deeds in the gentleness of wisdom.

JAMES 3:13 NASB

When pride comes, then comes shame; but with the humble is wisdom.

PROVERBS 11:2 NKJV

[You] should be gentle and kind to everyone.

TITUS 3:2 CEV

Everything He [God] does is right, and he does it the right way. He knows how to turn a proud person into a humble man or woman.

DANIEL 4:37 THE MESSAGE

Seek the LORD, all you meek of the earth, who have upheld His justice. Seek righteousness, seek humility. It may be that you will be hidden in the day of the LORD's anger.

ZEPHANIAH 2:3 NKJV

No, O people, the LORD has already told you what is good, and this is what he requires: to do what is right, to love mercy, and to walk humbly with your God.

MICAH 6:8 NLT

I [Paul] served the Lord with great humility and with tears, although I was severely tested by the plots of the Jews.

ACTS 20:19 NIV

Some time ago you decided to get understanding and to humble yourself before your God.

DANIEL 10:12 NCV

It was pride that changed angels into devils; it is humility that makes men as angels.

—SAINT AUGUSTINE

What makes humility so desirable is the marvelous thing it does to us; it creates in us a capacity for the closest possible intimacy with God.

—MONICA BALDWIN

Problem Solving

Solutions Through Service

That their hearts may be encouraged, having been knit together in love, and attaining to all the wealth that comes from the full assurance of understanding, resulting in a true knowledge of God's mystery, that is, Christ Himself, in whom are hidden all the treasures of wisdom and knowledge.

—COLOSSIANS 2:2–3 NASB

Joann took satisfaction from knowing her adult Bible class grew from week to week. When the class got too large the Sunday school superintendent approached her with a suggestion: Would she spin off two smaller classes, select teachers for each, and oversee their progress throughout the year, while teaching her own class? Joann accepted the challenge with enthusiasm and applied her people skills to the task. But by midyear the teaching group hit a snag. One of the teachers tried to do too much in too little time, spreading herself—and her class instruction—too thin. As complaints trickled in about the teacher's lack of preparation, Joann realized she had to do something.

Problem solving is as much a part of leadership as vision casting but proves to be far more troublesome. When problems surface, those you lead look to you for solutions—and you're expected to deliver. Stripped to its essence, problem solving is a positive activity, not a negative one. When you approach it as an opportunity to find a solution, the "problem" becomes a catalyst for creative thinking, a chance to apply wisdom where it is needed.

Aware that many business books talk about the leadership style of Jesus, Joann decided to go right to the source—the Bible—and study what Jesus did when problems sprang up among His disciples. He had to deal with diverse personalities, battle egos and insecurities, correct laziness, qualm fears, settle disputes, encourage bravery, and instill godly thinking. Along the way He molded those twelve men into a team that would one day turn the world upside down.

Joann noted that Jesus did something else in His leadership: Rather than "lord" it over those He led, He served them. When problems arose, He found creative solutions, such as feeding a crowd of hungry people with the food available rather than sending them away. Jesus demonstrated that a leader solves problems through service to those he or she leads.

Encouraged by what she read, Joann recruited a volunteer to handle the busy work for the overworked teacher, and she offered to team-teach for the next several weeks. She found tools on the Internet to help streamline the teaching process and encouraged the teacher to use them. By quarter's end, the teacher was back in the groove and confident about her teaching ability.

As you apply creative thinking to the task of problem solving, don't forget the most important step of all: prayer. Ask God for wisdom as you seek solutions to the issues that crop up. He will surprise you with His answers.

I Will

Ask God for wisdom in problem solving today.   *yes*   *no*

View problems as opportunities to find creative solutions.   *yes*   *no*

Keep my eyes open for examples of successful problem solving in my business community.   *yes*   *no*

Resolve to bring solutions through service, not by making demands.   *yes*   *no*

Meditate on why Jesus' style of problem solving was so successful.   *yes*   *no*

Endeavor to be a leader who models creative problem solving for others.   *yes*   *no*

Things to Do

☐ *Reread the Gospel of Mark and tally the number of times Jesus solved a problem through service.*

☐ *Read a book on creative problem solving, such as* 101 Creative Problem Solving Techniques *by James M. Higgins.*

☐ *Identify the biggest problem on your plate right now, and give yourself a definitive timeline for solving it.*

☐ *Block out an hour in your day, minimize distractions, and jot down several possible scenarios for solutions.*

☐ *Jump-start your problem-solving creativity by finding a solution to a small problem today. It will encourage you for the biggies.*

☐ *Ask yourself, "What would Jesus do in this situation?" and do it.*

Things to Remember

Give to Your servant an understanding heart to judge Your people, that I may discern between good and evil. For who is able to judge this great people of Yours?

1 KINGS 3:9 NKJV

[Jesus] said to his disciples, "The harvest is plentiful but the workers are few. Ask the Lord of the harvest, therefore, to send out workers into his harvest field."

MATTHEW 9:37–38 NIV

I decided there is nothing better than to enjoy food and drink and to find satisfaction in work. Then I realized that this pleasure is from the hand of God.

ECCLESIASTES 2:24 NLT

I'll make you wiser than anyone who has ever lived or ever will live.

1 KINGS 3:12 CEV

To man He [God] said, "Behold, the fear of the Lord, that is wisdom, and to depart from evil is understanding."

JOB 28:28 NKJV

Then I saw that wisdom excels folly as light excels darkness.

ECCLESIASTES 2:13 NKJV

Courage means to keep working a relationship, to continue seeking solutions to difficult problems, and to stay focused during stressful periods.

—DENIS WAITLEY

The leader seeks to communicate his vision to his followers. He captures their attention with his optimistic intuition of possible solutions to their needs. . . . He demonstrates confidence that the challenge can be met, the need resolved, the crisis overcome.

—JOHN HAGGAI

Letting Go

Releasing Your Grip

[Jesus said:] "Whoever desires to save his life will lose it,
but whoever loses his life for My sake will find it."
—MATTHEW 16:25 NKJV

Nobody had to teach David the fine art of control. It came
naturally, and he discovered he had a knack for making things
hum along like fine-tuned machinery—provided he micromanaged every step of the way. The only problem: He started
to alienate his team members in the process. Now his
challenge was learning to relinquish control while trusting
God (and his team members) to keep everything moving
smoothly.

As a leader you may walk the tightrope of control versus
letting go every day, and it's a balancing act that requires your
best effort. Apply too much pressure and those you lead cry
foul; relinquish too much responsibility and things go
undone—or fall apart completely. What's the secret to striking
a balance between the two?

Celebrated leaders of every discipline, from business and
politics to sports and ministry, possess the ability to inspire
others to effective action while maintaining a light touch. Like
a skilled rider who knows his horse well, the wise leader guides

through a combination of clear-cut training, decisive action, and trusting relinquishment.

No leader throughout history demonstrated this three-pronged approach better than Jesus. He taught His followers patiently, led by example, and then charged them with a mission and left the results up to them. But at no time during or after His life on earth did they question who was in charge. Jesus was undeniably the leader, the commander-in-chief. For all those who follow in His steps, He hints at this paradox of letting go when He says, "For whoever desires to save his life will lose it, but whoever loses his life for My sake will find it" (Matthew 16:25 NKJV).

To find the right balance in leadership, David introduced a new project that required intensive training. After coaching his team, he modeled the behavior he hoped to elicit and then set them free. The act of relinquishment felt like tiptoeing on a wobbly tree limb, but David knew he had to try. The results were worth it. Relieved of the heavy-handed management style, the team took their mission seriously and performed well. At the same time, David discovered a powerful leadership secret: People respond best when expected to do their best.

Look for ways you too can lead and then let go.

I Will

Release my grip in areas where I exert too much control.   yes ___   no ___

Model Christlike leadership as I teach and then trust those I lead to do the task.   yes ___   no ___

Pray for wisdom in discerning when to relinquish control of a situation.   yes ___   no ___

Meditate on what it means to "lose" something so that I might "gain" it.   yes ___   no ___

Inspire those I lead to learn the paradox of letting go.   yes ___   no ___

Turn micromanaged tasks into opportunities for growth in relinquishment.   yes ___   no ___

Things to Do

- [ ] *Pinpoint one project or situation over which you need to relinquish control, and do so.*

- [ ] *Mark a date on your calendar every month to practice letting go, and start with something small.*

- [ ] *Read a book about the art of relinquishing control, such as* Going to Pieces Without Falling Apart *by Mark Epstein.*

- [ ] *Network with others in your community or industry who balance leadership/relinquishment, and emulate their behavior.*

- [ ] *Ask those you lead for feedback on how well you release your grip, and follow up on suggestions.*

- [ ] *Charge those you lead with a mission this week, and make a conscious decision to trust their ability to do it.*

Things to Remember

Stop trusting in man, who has but a breath in his nostrils. Of what account is he?

ISAIAH 2:22 NIV

Anyone who trusts in him [Jesus Christ] will never be disappointed.

1 PETER 2:6 NCV

It is good that one should hope and wait quietly for the salvation of the LORD.

LAMENTATIONS 3:26 NKJV

The children of Israel were subdued at that time; and the children of Judah prevailed, because they relied on the LORD God of their fathers.

2 CHRONICLES 13:18 NKJV

I've hung on you from the day of my birth, the day you took me from the cradle; I'll never run out of praise.

PSALM 71:6 THE MESSAGE

Hear my prayer, O LORD, give ear to my supplications! Answer me in Your faithfulness, in Your righteousness!

PSALM 143:1 NASB

Your ability to learn depends partly on your ability to relinquish what you've held.
—MILTON HALL

When you become detached mentally from yourself and concentrate on helping other people with their difficulties, you will be able to cope with your own more effectively. Somehow, the act of self-giving is a personal power-releasing factor.
— NORMAN VINCENT PEALE

Perseverance

Staying the Course

Without wavering, let us hold tightly to the hope we say we have, for God can be trusted to keep his promise.
—HEBREWS 10:23 NLT

The day Ethan first set foot on the college campus, he told his best friend Matt he would be class president before he graduated. Matt smiled knowingly and dismissed his friend's words. Ethan was always talking big, but nobody put much stake in it.

Still, Matt couldn't help but notice Ethan's determination throughout their freshman year as he joined one student organization after another. Ethan volunteered for activities no other students seemed to want to do and studied hard to keep his grade point average high.

Every evening in the dorm, Matt also noticed Ethan poring over one book in particular—the Bible. He closed his study session on his knees, asking God to make him diligent and to bless his efforts. During their sophomore year, Ethan ran for the student government and lost. Seeing his friend's discouragement, Matt told Ethan to let it go and focus on his studies, but Ethan wouldn't accept failure. He plodded on, losing two other elections. In his senior year he finally was elected class president and made reforms that earned him a spot among the university's most memorable class presidents.

Perseverance—it's a twelve-letter word that contains the power to change your leadership career from mediocre to memorable. It also finds long precedence in God's Word. Think of any Bible hero, and you'll have a picture of perseverance personified. Abraham waited a quarter century for the fulfillment of God's promise of a son; Jacob worked seven years to win Rachel as a bride, then got tricked into working another seven years; Joseph spent years in an Egyptian prison before God raised him to a position of prominence in the empire.

God puts a high premium on perseverance, regardless of the title you go by. Several of Jesus' parables are about godly persistence, and the second half of Hebrews 10 issues a call to perseverance: "Let us hold unswervingly to the hope we profess, for he who promised is faithful. And let us consider how we may spur one another on toward love and good deeds. . . . So do not throw away your confidence; it will be richly rewarded. You need to persevere so that when you have done the will of God, you will receive what he has promised" (Hebrews 10:23–24, 35–36 NIV).

Perhaps your organization is struggling financially, and it falls to you to bring it out of the red and into the black. The combined task of wise leadership and careful stewardship will require perseverance on your part. Maybe you face competition so stiff you would be tempted to despair—if not for a dogged determination to plod onward. Whatever situation you face in your leadership role, realize that the perseverance you apply today will reap long-range benefits. As you commit to be the tortoise rather than the hare, your organization will take steps in the direction of success, because perseverance brings reward.

The son of a British author, Benjamin Disraeli trained to be a solicitor in nineteenth-century England, but his real aspirations lay in politics. In the early 1830s he took part in several elections, but all of them ended in failure. He eventually got elected to the House of Commons in 1837, and when his maiden speech earned him ridicule by his peers, Disraeli said, "Though I sit down now, the time will come when you will hear me."

Over the ensuring years, Disraeli won and subsequently lost several political positions until finally, in 1868, he was elected prime minister of England. He became a favorite of Queen Victoria and earned acclaim for his efforts to improve conditions for the poor and working class. His perseverance made all the difference between the life he could have lived as an obscure solicitor and the life he was destined to lead as the head of a nation.

What about you? What calling has God placed on your life? Perhaps He is just beginning to reveal His divine purpose for your life, or steering you into an entirely different direction than the one you intended to take. As you seek His grace and favor and direction in leadership, do your best to persevere. It will make all the difference.

I Will

Focus on God, not on the obstacles in my
leadership path.   *yes*   *no*

Adopt a tortoise mentality in the race of life.   *yes*   *no*

Meditate on what it means to persevere in the face
of setbacks and daily difficulties.   *yes*   *no*

Realize that perseverance and faith go hand-in-hand
(as they did for the Bible heroes).   *yes*   *no*

Ask God for the strength to hang in there when I
lose momentum.   *yes*   *no*

Act on the will to persevere, not wait for
"inspiration" to do so.   *yes*   *no*

Things to Do

- [ ] *Identify the biggest obstacles to success in your leadership, and brainstorm ways to overcome them.*

- [ ] *Jot down a short list of ways you have persevered through the years, with God's help.*

- [ ] *Look for examples of perseverance in those you lead, and reward their efforts.*

- [ ] *Read* Waking the Dead: The Glory of a Heart Fully Alive *by John Eldredge and apply its wisdom to perseverance in leadership.*

- [ ] *Define perseverance as it applies to your leadership situation right now.*

- [ ] *Find a mentor who is willing to keep you accountable in perseverance training.*

Things to Remember

Let us not grow weary while doing good, for in due season we shall reap if we do not lose heart.

GALATIANS 6:9 NKJV

Look to yourselves, that we do not lose those things we worked for, but that we may receive a full reward.

2 JOHN 1:8 NKJV

Our motive for writing is simply this: We want you to enjoy this, too. Your joy will double our joy!

1 John 1:4 THE MESSAGE

Everyone will hate you because of me. But if you remain faithful until the end, you will be saved.

MATTHEW 10:22 CEV

Do not be afraid of what you are about to suffer. I tell you, the devil will put some of you in prison to test you, and you will suffer persecution for ten days. Be faithful, even to the point of death, and I will give you the crown of life.

REVELATION 2:10 NIV

Be sure you continue to follow the teaching you heard from the beginning. If you continue to follow what you heard from the beginning, you will stay in the Son and in the Father.

1 JOHN 2:24 NCV

If you abide in Me, and My words abide in you, you will ask what you desire, and it shall be done for you.

JOHN 15:7 NKJV

He who has a slack hand becomes poor, but the hand of the diligent makes rich.

PROVERBS 10:4 NKJV

Hard work always pays off; mere talk puts no bread on the table.

PROVERBS 14:23 THE MESSAGE

Good planning and hard work lead to prosperity, but hasty shortcuts lead to poverty.

PROVERBS 21:5 NLT

Whoever has, to him more shall be given, and he will have an abundance; but whoever does not have, even what he has shall be taken away from him.

MATTHEW 13:12 NASB

Do you see a man who excels in his work? He will stand before kings; he will not stand before unknown men.

PROVERBS 22:29 NKJV

He who works his land will have abundant food, but the one who chases fantasies will have his fill of poverty.

PROVERBS 28:19 NIV

Courage and perseverance have a magical talisman, before which difficulties disappear and obstacles vanish into air.

—JOHN QUINCY ADAMS

If your determination is fixed, I do not counsel you to despair. Few things are impossible to diligence and skill. Great works are performed not by strength, but perseverance.

—SAMUEL JOHNSON

Hope

The Eternal Spring

*I have set the LORD always before me; because He is at my
right hand I shall not be moved. Therefore my heart is glad,
and my glory rejoices; My flesh also will rest in hope.*

—PSALM 16:8–9 NKJV

When an affordable new exercise franchise emerged on the
market, Devon realized her chance for business success might
have come at last. A fitness buff, she regarded the franchise as a
perfect fit for her business and personal goals. Within six
months she opened the business and saw immediate success.
The franchise name alone drew in customers, and Devon
watched her bank account climb.

Two years later, however, she noticed a drop-off in both
member attendance and new memberships. The franchise,
once a household word, was proving to be a fad, and now
Devon worried about the future of her business—as well as her
capital reserves. What would she do if the business went belly-
up?

Devon confided in a friend about her fears and asked her
advice. The friend startled Devon by asking if she had talked to
God about the situation. In all her worries, Devon had
neglected her most important resource—her hope in the Lord.
Together with her friend, Devon committed her business and

finances to God and asked Him to restore her faith and hope in Him. She reminded herself anew of His promise to work everything out for good as she put Him first in her life.

Hope, indeed, is one of your prize assets as a godly leader. Without it, your leadership and organization would suffer loss. But when you exercise hope and express it openly to those you lead, you'll see their spirits lift as well.

One leader who faced overwhelming trials—including death threats—encouraged his spirit continually by hoping in God. He was so fastened on God's goodness in the midst of troubles that his words of hope became part of Scripture. David, the shepherd not-yet king, set his hope, his safety, and his life in God's hands and left them there. He not only hoped in God but vocalized his hope, which served to boost his flagging spirit.

Think for a moment about the people you lead and the organization God has placed under your care. Make a mental list of all the things that worry you about your leadership role. It could be a difficult person, your company's balance sheet, deadlines that loom near—you name it. Now, one by one reframe those worries into scenarios of hope.

As you face the pressures of leadership today, set your hope securely in the One who promised never to leave you or forsake you.

I Will

Meditate on the words of Psalm 25.   yes _____   no _____

Remind myself to trust and hope in God, even when   yes _____   no _____
things are going well.

Maintain an attitude of inward prayer at all times.   yes _____   no _____

Turn my worries over to God and ask Him to replace   yes _____   no _____
them with hope.

Strive to be a hopeful person in the presence of   yes _____   no _____
those I lead.

Instill hope in the people I influence.   yes _____   no _____

Things to Do

☐ *Read a book on keeping positive and hopeful, such as* The Power of
Positive Thinking *by Norman Vincent Peale.*

☐ *Get reacquainted with God in daily take-five breaks to rejuvenate your
hope in Him.*

☐ *Create a visual reminder, such as an acronym for HOPE, and place it
where you will see it daily.*

☐ *Skim through your appointment book or prayer journal from last year
to see how many times God came through for you.*

☐ *Quote a favorite psalm out loud to bolster a flagging spirit or raise
your hopes.*

☐ *Trade anecdotes about hoping in God with a like-minded colleague.*

Things to Remember

Why am I discouraged? Why so sad? I will put my hope in God! I will praise him again—my Savior and my God!

PSALM 42:11 NLT

This hope we have as an anchor of the soul, both sure and steadfast, and which enters the Presence behind the veil.

HEBREWS 6:19 NKJV

Blessed be the God and Father of our Lord Jesus Christ, who according to His abundant mercy has begotten us again to a living hope through the resurrection of Jesus Christ from the dead.

1 PETER 1:3 NKJV

I depend on you, and I have trusted you since I was young.

PSALM 71:5 CEV

Christ is pure, and all who have this hope in Christ keep themselves pure like Christ.

1 JOHN 3:3 NCV

Take my side as you promised; I'll live then for sure. Don't disappoint all my grand hopes.

PSALM 119:116 THE MESSAGE

Hope is the parent of faith.

—CYRUS A. BARTOL

Before you give up hope, turn back and read the attacks that were made on Lincoln.

—BRUCE BARTON

Focus

Bull's-Eye

[Jesus said:] "Enter through the narrow gate; for the gate is wide and the way is broad that leads to destruction, and there are many who enter through it."

—Matthew 7:13 NASB

Kate called a meeting and congratulated her team on reaching an important goal. Together, they had worked for the past year toward acquiring a large account, and they had done it. As she toasted the group, a thought ran through her head: *Now that we won the contract, we have to deliver. We must create an ad campaign worthy of Madison Avenue.* Kate knew that by keeping her focus on the bull's eye—the big-picture purpose that defined what her agency was all about—the business would stay on track and remain true to its mission statement to develop top-notch advertising that sold products and changed lives.

As a leader, you are your organization's visionary, the one who keeps an eye on the far horizon while creating today's solutions. Skilled archers can hit the target every time and the bull's-eye much of the time. By keeping their focus trained on the right point, their accuracy increases. In like manner, by keeping your focus on the big-picture goal, you increase your organization's chances of success and propel those you lead toward quality performance.

Focus as a leadership trait is closely tied to ambition, for only by keeping your eye on the goal will you build momentum to carry your organization forward. Our English word *ambition* comes from two Latin words: *ambi,* which means "about," and *itum,* which means "to go." Together, the two words denote an intense longing that motivates a person to go out of their way to achieve it.

Before his life-changing encounter on the Damascus Road, Saul (later called Paul) was driven by a sole purpose: to persecute followers of The Way, a new religion that threatened centuries of Jewish tradition. But after his dramatic run-in with the risen Christ, his ambition—his focus—took a 180-degree turn. Paul redirected his passion toward serving God by making converts to Christianity everywhere he went. So single-minded was his purpose that he later wrote to the Philippians, "Forgetting what is behind and straining toward what is ahead, I press on toward the goal to win the prize for which God has called me heavenward in Christ Jesus" (Philippians 3:13–14 NIV). His zeal never changed; his focus changed entirely.

The people you lead are looking to you to set a clear-cut focus. They take their cues from you, watching to see how you maintain a course direction for the organization. As you keep your focus on the big-picture goal, you communicate security, purpose, and a renewed sense of ambition.

I Will

Keep my eyes on the big-picture purpose of my organization.

yes _no_

Realize that I am responsible for my organization's focus.

yes _no_

Pay attention to areas in which I may have veered off track from my original goals.

yes _no_

Meditate on the archer analogy and strive to hit the target every time.

yes _no_

Communicate a sense of direction to those I lead.

yes _no_

Believe that my leadership focus fuels momentum for the future.

yes _no_

Things to Do

☐ _Ask God to give you a clear-cut focus for your organization._

☐ _E-mail a concise description of your organization's purpose, as you understand it right now, to those you lead._

☐ _Make a list of ways in which you may have lost focus, and brainstorm ideas for getting back on track._

☐ _Discover more about keeping focused by reading_ The Power of Focus _by Jack Canfield._

☐ _Enlist the help of those you lead to draft individual goals for each person._

☐ _Reconnect this week with someone who exudes a sense of mission and purpose._

Things to Remember

Let your eyes look straight ahead, fix your gaze directly before you.

PROVERBS 4:25 NIV

Behold, God is my salvation, I will trust and not be afraid; for YAH, the LORD, is my strength and song; He also has become my salvation.

ISAIAH 12:2 NKJV

Then your face will brighten in innocence. You will be strong and free of fear.

JOB 11:15 NLT

Don't make a mistake by turning to the right or the left.

PROVERBS 4:27 CEV

While we do not look at the things which are seen, but at the things which are not seen. For the things which are seen are temporary, but the things which are not seen are eternal.

2 CORINTHIANS 4:18 NKJV

Folly is joy to him who lacks sense, but a man of understanding walks straight.

PROVERBS 15:21 NASB

You must remain focused on your journey to greatness.

—LES BROWN

To me, the definition of focus is knowing exactly where you want to be today, next week, next month, next year, then never deviating from your plan. Once you can see, touch and feel your objective, all you have to do is pull back and put all your strength behind it, and you'll hit your target every time.

—BRUCE JENNER

Time Management

Minute-Minder

To every thing there is a season, and a time to every purpose under the heaven.

—ECCLESIASTES 3:1 KJV

The harder he worked, the less he seemed to accomplish, Brian thought as he studied his department's project overview for month-end. Sure, he stayed busy and put out fires daily, but somehow the big things fell prey to the tyranny of the urgent. As a manager, he knew the corporate leaders expected him to provide solutions for his department, but he didn't want to appear inefficient by asking for help. Instead, he sought counsel from a business mentor he met through a networking organization.

At his friend's suggestion, Brian asked his staff to keep time sheets to record their work activities for two weeks. He blocked segments of time on the department calendar and challenged his staff to regard those segments as sacred hours— no interruptions. Next he cut out unnecessary meetings and made better use of e-mail rather than the telephone. But the most important thing he did was to take God's view of time seriously.

Thousands of years ago, a wise leader wrote, "There is a time for everything, and a season for every activity under heaven" (Ecclesiastes 3:1 NIV). Though Solomon didn't have corporate workdays in mind when he penned these words, they apply to your situation regardless of the leadership role you fulfill. Skip over to the New Testament, and you'll see words from another leader about the wise use of time. Paul urged the church at Ephesus, "Be very careful, then, how you live—not as unwise but as wise, making the most of every opportunity" (Ephesians 5:15–16 NIV).

Why does God have such a vested interest in how you use your time? The key to that answer is found in His passion for people, His zeal for turning meaningless lives into implements of destiny. Every day, you are given a new opportunity to impact lives for better or for worse. Under your mantle the people you lead discover their own calling and purpose, and how you make use of the time you have with them is critical. Seen in that light, making the most of every opportunity means much more than minding minutes; it means taking the tool of time and using it to nudge men and women into their own God-given destinies.

As Brian came to see his leadership role as a divine calling—a mission field of sorts—he found a renewed sense of purpose and vigor on the job. He no longer just turned projects and logged time; he sculpted lives. As those he led caught his vision for time management, the department increased productivity. Morale picked up. The workplace buzzed with meaning.

One leader who took time management to the extreme lived a short life by today's standards but packed a full lifetime of accomplishment into his thirty-four years. While a chaplain at Oxford in the seventeenth century, Joseph Alleine often pored over his books to the neglect of his friends. "It is better they should wonder at my rudeness than that I should lose time," he said, "for only a few will notice my rudeness, but many will feel my loss of time." Alleine devoted every spare minute to studying, preaching, and evangelizing. He rose at 4:00 a.m. to pray and study the Bible, then spent his afternoons reaching the unconverted. "Give me a Christian that counts his time more precious than gold," he once said.

England's Act of Uniformity under the restored monarchy in 1662 removed two thousand preachers from their pulpits in a single day, but Alleine refused to stop preaching and landed in prison. Upon his release, he told his wife, "Now we have one day more. Let us live well, work hard for souls, lay up much treasure in heaven this day, for we have but a few to live." Alleine died shortly thereafter.

Only God knows how many days are allotted to you, but it's up to you to make those days—and the hours and minutes within them—count for eternity. Use time as a precious commodity, and learn to see those you lead as implements of destiny.

I Will

Place a high priority on the hours I'm given in
each day.

yes _____ _no_ _____

Realize that the people I lead are my
"mission field."

yes _____ _no_ _____

Be aware of time wasters in my daily activities.

yes _____ _no_ _____

Commit to spend time with God each day to renew
my leadership vision.

yes _____ _no_ _____

Make the most of whatever time I have left on earth,
counting it as "gold."

yes _____ _no_ _____

Model good time management for those I lead.

yes _____ _no_ _____

Things to Do

☐ _Memorize Ephesians 5:16–17._

☐ _Keep a time sheet of daily activities, noting repeated time wasters that
creep into your schedule._

☐ _Make a list of your time wasters, and eliminate one a week until the
list is cleared._

☐ _Meet with a mentor to glean wisdom about time management._

☐ _Make better use of e-mail; use the telephone only when necessary._

☐ _Cancel unnecessary meetings and keep required meetings short and
to-the-point._

☐ _Block out no-interruption times on your daily schedule._

Things to Remember

What I mean, brothers, is that the time is short.

1 CORINTHIANS 7:29 NIV

Christ arrives right on time to make this happen. He didn't, and doesn't, wait for us to get ready. He presented himself for this sacrificial death when we were far too weak and rebellious to do anything to get ourselves ready.

ROMANS 5:6 THE MESSAGE

> *My life is in your hands. Save me from my enemies and from those who are chasing me.*
> Psalm 31:15 NCV

Sow for yourselves righteousness; reap in mercy; break up your fallow ground, for it is time to seek the LORD, till He comes and rains righteousness on you.

HOSEA 10:12 NKJV

When the fullness of the time had come, God sent forth His Son, born of a woman, born under the law.

GALATIANS 4:4 NKJV

Therefore let him who thinks he stands take heed lest he fall.

1 CORINTHIANS 10:12 NKJV

Therefore, be on the alert—for you do not know when the master of the house is coming, whether in the evening, at midnight, or when the rooster crows, or in the morning.

MARK 13:35 NASB

"Take note: I [Jesus] will come as
unexpectedly as a thief! Blessed are all
who are watching for me, who keep
their robes ready so they will not need
to walk naked and ashamed."

REVELATION 16:15 NLT

Don't get ahead of the Master and jump
to conclusions with your judgments
before all the evidence is in. When he
comes, he will bring out in the open
and place in evidence all kinds of things
we never even dreamed of—inner
motives and purposes and prayers. Only
then will any one of us get to hear the
"Well done!" of God.

1 CORINTHIANS 4:5 THE MESSAGE

Remember, therefore, what you have
received and heard; obey it, and repent.
But if you do not wake up, I will come
like a thief, and you will not know at
what time I will come to you.

REVELATION 3:3 NIV

I stay awake all night so I can think
about your promises.

PSALM 119:148 NCV

He that observeth the wind shall not
sow; and he that regardeth the clouds
shall not reap.

ECCLESIASTES 11:4 KJV

Since time is the
one immaterial
object which we
cannot influence —
neither speed up
nor slow down, add
to nor diminish —
it is an
imponderably
valuable gift.

—MAYA ANGELOU

Time is the
measure of
business.

—FRANCIS BACON

Courage

Be Bold and Courageous!

*Keep your eyes open, hold tight to your convictions, give it
all you've got, be resolute.*

—1 CORINTHIANS 16:13 THE MESSAGE

In the past, John always relied on the weight of his
business credentials to give him credibility. He was proud of
his stature in the business community and enjoyed the perks it
afforded him. But his company had gone under amid rumors
of a scandal, and now John stood before a group as a wiser but
broken man—and the newly appointed leader of a men's
organization. As he stepped to the podium, he asked God for
the courage to speak boldly and honestly, knowing that the
men gathered would look to him for character-building
guidance as they struggled to live godly lives in a godless
world.

Courage can be summed up as the moral backbone that
separates true leaders from posers. God places this character
trait high on the list of worthy pursuits, and the heroes of faith
summoned courage against unspeakable odds. Three times
God said to Joshua, "Be strong and courageous" as he prepared
to take the Israelites into Canaan. God backed up His words
with a promise: "Do not be terrified; do not be discouraged,
for the LORD your God will be with you wherever you go"

(Joshua 1:9 NIV). Armed with that promise, Joshua led the campaign to take the land of Canaan and met success. Given the situation, he had every right to be discouraged, but he chose to take courage in the Lord instead.

The word *discourage* literally means to deprive of courage or confidence, to dishearten. No wonder God calls His people to be encouragers—those who build up courage and confidence in others. Like Joshua, a godly leader takes his or her confidence from God and spreads it to others. But how do you make this work in the real world? John had the right idea by going directly to the Source in a moment of insecurity and doubt. The same privilege is available to you.

History records the story of a courageous leader in the early church who took a bold stand that cost him his life. Trained in ministry by the apostle John, Polycarp pastored the church in Smyrna and battled heresy throughout the Roman empire. He faced his greatest trial when Rome launched a widespread persecution against Christians and demanded that he renounce Christ. The old pastor replied, "Eighty and six years have I served Him and He has done me no wrong. Can I revile my King that saved me?"

God has set a leadership mission before you and charged you with the task of leading well. As you encounter discouraging odds and bleak situations, ask Him for the courage to press on. His promise to Joshua holds true for you too.

I Will

Ask God for courage in my leadership role.
yes   no

Believe that I can be strong and courageous with God directing my steps.
yes   no

Replace negative thoughts with positive affirmations from Scripture, such as Joshua 1:9.
yes   no

Realize that those I lead look to me for an example of courage in action.
yes   no

Expect God to enable me for the task of leading to which He called me.
yes   no

Think of ways I can encourage those who are discouraged.
yes   no

Understand that true confidence comes from God.
yes   no

Things to Do

☐ *Make a list of all the things you could do if you really believed Philippians 4:13.*

☐ *Read* Courageous Leadership *by Bill Hybels and jot down five things you can do to increase your courage in leadership.*

☐ *Ask God to forgive you for lacking courage—essentially distrusting Him—in the past.*

☐ *Pick a daunting task, pray for courage, then do it with the confidence that God is on your side.*

☐ *Ask a friend for an anecdote about a time they needed courage, and found it. Glean wisdom from their story.*

☐ *Read Joshua 1 and put yourself in Joshua's position. How would you feel after hearing God's commands?*

Things to Remember

Be strong and courageous. Do not be afraid or terrified because of them, for the LORD your God goes with you; he will never leave you nor forsake you.

DEUTERONOMY 31:6 NIV

If you carefully obey the laws and regulations that the LORD gave to Israel through Moses, you will be successful. Be strong and courageous; do not be afraid or lose heart!

1 CHRONICLES 22:13 NLT

Can your heart endure, or can your hands remain strong, in the days when I shall deal with you? I, the LORD, have spoken, and will do it.

EZEKIEL 22:14 NKJV

Christ as Son is in charge of the house. Now, if we can only keep a firm grip on this bold confidence, we're the house!

HEBREWS 3:6 THE MESSAGE

I urge you to take heart, for there will be no loss of life among you, but only of the ship.

ACTS 27:22 NKJV

Only be strong and very courageous, that you may observe to do according to all the law which Moses My servant commanded you; do not turn from it to the right hand or to the left, that you may prosper wherever you go.

JOSHUA 1:7 NKJV

Often the test of courage is not to die but to live.

—CONTE DI ALFIERI VITTORIO

It takes a lot of courage to show your dreams to someone else.

—ERMA BOMBECK

Gratitude

The Simplest Word

*Every creature of God is good, and nothing is to be refused
if it is received with thanksgiving.*

—1 TIMOTHY 4:4 NKJV

The batter from the opposing team hit a pop fly, and
Fletcher held his breath as he waited to see if the outfielder
would catch it. He did. Fletcher, along with every parent sitting
in the home-team bleachers, breathed a sigh of relief followed
by a roaring cheer. As the boys rushed in from the field with
their third out, Fletcher said a silent prayer of thanks and
reminded himself again why he loved this game—and the boys
he was privileged to coach.

Later that afternoon, after the game, one father
approached Fletcher with his hand extended. "I never stopped
to thank you for all the hard work you do for these boys, but it
shows," the man said. Fletcher blinked and told the man he
was honored to work with his son. As the man walked away,
Fletcher couldn't help but picture God smiling from heaven—
the gratitude had been returned.

Have you ever stopped and thanked God for the people
you lead? At times, no doubt, they cause you great frustration,
but the simple awareness that leadership is a privilege will help

lift your job into the ranks of a calling. Gratitude is an underrated—and disappearing—commodity in today's world, yet wise leaders know it to be a powerful motivator. An attitude of constant thankfulness smooths over misunderstandings and spreads peace in its wake.

One individual who found herself in unexpected leadership turned gratitude into a daily provision of grace. When Maria Augusta Kutschera first accepted the job of governess to a retired naval captain's children, she never imagined her life would change beyond recognition. The children she oversaw proved to be more than a handful, challenging her leadership at every turn. In a memorable scene from *The Sound of Music*, the motion picture story of her life, Maria kneels by her bed and thanks God for each of the seven children—some mischievous, some abominable, some sweet. She finds something to thank God for in each child, even when it stretches her imagination. Those same children, in turn, become the means for her greatest blessing in life as she assumes the roles of wife to the captain and beloved stepmother to the motherless children.

Thanks is a simple word, and as a leader you can't say it enough. Remind yourself of the blessings your leadership role bestows every day.

I Will

Be thankful for those under my leadership. _yes_ _no_

Meditate on what it means to be a leader of gratitude in a thankless world. _yes_ _no_

Look for traits to be thankful for in those who frustrate me the most. _yes_ _no_

Verbalize thanks; don't just think it. _yes_ _no_

Realize that my gratitude is a positive witness for Christ. _yes_ _no_

Encourage gratitude in those I lead. _yes_ _no_

Confess any act of ungratefulness on my part. _yes_ _no_

Things to Do

☐ Read Psalm 118 and meditate on why the psalmist is so thankful.

☐ Make a list of things you are thankful for today that you weren't thankful for one year ago.

☐ Build "thanks!" into your leadership vocabulary, and say it several times a day.

☐ Think of two or three people who frustrate you; then think of a positive trait you can be thankful for in each.

☐ Model gratitude as you go about your leadership tasks today.

☐ Read The Power of Appreciation by Noelle C. Nelson and Jeannine Lemare Calaba, and compare and contrast takeaway points to your own life.

Things to Remember

Let the teaching of Christ live in you richly. Use all wisdom to teach and instruct each other by singing psalms, hymns, and spiritual songs with thankfulness in your hearts to God.

COLOSSIANS 3:16 NCV

Since we are receiving a kingdom that cannot be shaken, let us be thankful, and so worship God acceptably with reverence and awe.

HEBREWS 12:28 NIV

In everything give thanks; for this is the will of God in Christ Jesus for you.

1 THESSALONIANS 5:18 NKJV

I will sacrifice to You with the voice of thanksgiving; I will pay what I have vowed. Salvation is of the LORD.

JONAH 2:9 NKJV

Come to worship him with thankful hearts and songs of praise.

PSALM 95:2 CEV

Thank the God of all gods, His love never quits.

PSALM 136:2 THE MESSAGE

Gratitude is not only the greatest of virtues, but the parent of all the others.

—MARCUS T. CICERO

One can never pay in gratitude; one can only pay "in kind" somewhere else in life.

—ANNE MORROW LINDBERGH

Empowerment

Freeing Your Followers

[John wrote:] *Dear children, let us not love with words or tongue but with actions and in truth.*

—1 John 3:18 NIV

Some people said Samantha opened her office-park deli at the worst possible time. The economy was slow, two rival eateries claimed real estate space in the park, and one large business had just moved across town, leaving an entire building vacant. But Samantha looked at her business plan and fledgling staff through a different lens. By featuring all-organic foods and a delivery service to the office-park clients, she offered them something special. To empower her staff, she allowed them to create a bonus system for counter sales and encouraged their creative touch on filling lunch orders. The fact that they devised the bonus system gave her employees a sense of ownership, and sales took off.

People flourish when they are expected to do their best and given the tools to make it happen. Empowerment means enabling someone to act on the mission you've set before them by clearly defining the goal, equipping them with the time and resources to get the job done, and urging them on through verbal affirmation and constructive feedback.

Take the analogy of a football coach. The team faces its biggest opponent in an upcoming game, and the coach knows this game will test his players to the limits of their ability. Undaunted, he states the goal clearly—winning the game— and fixes it in the minds of his players. Next he calls for three extra hours of practice a week to get the players in top form. He stretches the budget to make sure they have the best training equipment and hires a retired pro to talk to the team about excellence on the field. With the goal clearly in sight, the coach drills, corrects, and encourages the team through verbal affirmations. By the time the big night arrives, they hardly resemble the players they used to be. The team is empowered to win.

The biblical notion of empowerment can best be defined by the word *enabled*, which is another way of saying "equipped." David's song of praise to the Lord in 2 Samuel 22 claims, "For who is God besides the LORD? And who is the Rock except our God? It is God who arms me with strength and makes my way perfect. He makes my feet like the feet of a deer; he enables me to stand on the heights" (vv. 32–34 NIV). The book of Acts, recounting the Old Testament story of Joseph, states, "But God was with him and rescued him from all his troubles. He gave Joseph wisdom and enabled him to gain the goodwill of Pharaoh king of Egypt" (Acts 7:9–10 NIV).

While God is the One who empowers His people to fulfill their destinies, godly leaders play a role by coming alongside and equipping those they lead. It's possible to give your people all the training and tools in the world, but without setting them free to develop their abilities, you are not really empowering them. Conversely, you can shout encouragement all day, but unless you equip them with the necessary resources, they won't achieve their best performance. This duel-edged sword of empowerment is most effectively wielded by leaders who understand God's view of enabling, for here a third component comes into play: the supernatural work of God.

When the people you lead realize God is working through them and through you, as their leader, something remarkable happens. An indefinable spark ignites the workplace with purpose and passion. A sense of camaraderie and teamwork emerges.

Samantha did more than enable her deli employees to succeed. She communicated her vision for excellence as a personal life goal to honor God through her work. Those glowing words would have amounted to nothing if she hadn't backed them up with actions. Instead of Bible-thumping, she lived out the spirit of the two great commandments Jesus taught (love God and love people). Her employees saw her put their needs first; they watched her smile despite how she felt; they caught her contagious enthusiasm for the work; they enjoyed financial and verbal rewards for a job well done; and they noticed how pleasant she was to be around.

Look for ways you can empower those you lead, and never forget that your good example is the first step in the right direction.

I Will

Believe that God wants to work with me in empowering those I lead.

yes   _no_

Pray for direction and specific ideas on how to empower others.

yes   _no_

Pay attention to the strengths already present in those I lead, and think of ways to enhance them.

yes   _no_

Meditate on what it means to enable someone to be their best.

yes   _no_

Be aware of how my leadership mood helps or hinders those I serve.

yes   _no_

Things to Do

☐ _Identify your natural gifts for empowerment, and work on areas that need improvement._

☐ _Write a vision statement for how you would like to empower each individual you lead._

☐ _Research practical tools of empowerment that apply to your field of endeavor._

☐ _Read the section on "Enabling Others to Act" in_ The Leadership Challenge _by Jim Kouzes and Barry Posner._

☐ _Ask those you lead what resources would help them do a better job and feel a sense of ownership._

☐ _Hold an informal "round table" over lunch with other leaders, and find out how they empower those they lead._

Things to Remember

God did not give us a spirit of timidity, but a spirit of power, of love and of self-discipline.

2 TIMOTHY 1:7 NIV

Then he [Ananias] said, "The God of our fathers has chosen you that you should know His will, and see the Just One, and hear the voice of His mouth.

ACTS 22:14 NKJV

May the God of patience and comfort grant you to be like-minded toward one another, according to Christ Jesus.

Romans 15:5 NKJV

I [Paul] bow my knees to the Father of our Lord Jesus Christ.

EPHESIANS 3:14 NKJV

Freely you have received, freely give.

MATTHEW 10:8 NKJV

I will walk at liberty, for I seek Your precepts.

PSALM 119:45 NASB

To him who loves us and has freed us from our sins by his blood, and has made us to be a kingdom and priests to serve his God and Father—to him be glory and power for ever and ever! Amen.

REVELATION 1:5–6 NIV

If the Son makes you free, you shall be free indeed.

JOHN 8:36 NKJV

We have great joy and consolation in thy love, because the bowels of the saints are refreshed by thee, brother.

PHILEMON 1:7 KJV

Woodcarvers, goldsmiths, and other workers encourage one another and say, "We've done a great job!"

ISAIAH 41:7 CEV

Holding your hand, whispering encouragement, showing you step-by-step how to live well before God, who called us into his own kingdom, into this delightful life.

1 THESSALONIANS 2:12
THE MESSAGE

I wrote to encourage you and to tell you that this is the true grace of God. Stand strong in that grace.

1 PETER 5:12 NCV

It is essential that we enable young people to see themselves as participants in one of the most exciting eras in history, and to have a sense of purpose in relation to it.

—NELSON ROCKEFELLER

The purpose of life . . . is a life of purpose.

—AUTHOR UNKNOWN

Sacrifice

Less Is More

[Paul wrote:] And so, dear brothers and sisters, I plead with you to give your bodies to God. Let them be a living and holy sacrifice—the kind he will accept. When you think of what he has done for you, is this too much to ask?

—ROMANS 12:1 NLT

By the end of the third quarter, Joe realized he would have to do one of two things: cut the staff at his manufacturing plant or announce a company-wide pay cut. Otherwise, the company would end the year in the red. He decided to offer his workers a choice. As he announced the two options, he said he would trim his own salary by 15 percent while cutting their wages 3 percent. None of the workers knew how much Joe made, but they recognized an act of sacrifice when they saw it. They rallied around him and voted for the pay cut; no one got laid off. As an unexpected perk, the plant enjoyed boosted morale, and when profits picked up the following year Joe rewarded his employees with generous raises.

The concept of sacrifice originates with the symbolic atonement for sin by the shedding of blood. God took this concept to the extreme in the life (and sacrificial death) of Jesus, but in the leadership context sacrifice typically means something other than physical death. You may have encountered situations that called for sacrifices of time, money, or goals. Perhaps you had to sacrifice a cherished dream to realize a practical goal in the short term. Sacrifice, by its connotation, is not something you long for—it is always associated with loss. Yet it remains one of the central themes of the Bible, and God calls His followers to a life of sacrifice.

What does it mean to be a sacrificial leader? It starts with presenting yourself to God as a "living and holy sacrifice," a pure vessel He can use for His purposes. Imagine how difficult it would be for God to accomplish His plans for an organization through a selfish, prideful leader. Now contrast that with the leader who puts others before himself, seeks the highest good of those he serves, and takes care of the organization before looking to his own needs. Like the captain of a ship, a godly leader makes sure everyone else on board finds refuge in a lifeboat during a crisis at sea. His own life may be expendable.

The Poseidon Adventure, a 1970s disaster film starring Gene Hackman, shows just such a leader in action. As the ship is sinking, only a handful of survivors remain, and they must work together to find a way out of the ship. Hackman's character, a preacher, directs the group toward safety. When the band of survivors is only moments away from rescue, one last obstacle stands in their way. The preacher sacrifices his own life to shut off a steam valve that otherwise would kill those he led to safety.

Look for opportunities to be a sacrificial leader today. You may or may not be rewarded with boosted morale as Joe was, but sacrifice brings its own rewards.

I Will

Develop a heart of sacrificial service to those under
my leadership.

yes   *no*

Realize the cost of God's sacrifice for me.

yes   *no*

Remember that sacrifice is not an option for a
godly leader.

yes   *no*

Change my attitude from one of having to sacrifice
to one of getting to sacrifice.

yes   *no*

Define my leadership integrity by my willingness to
sacrifice for those I lead.

yes   *no*

Look for situations that call for sacrificial
leadership.

yes   *no*

Things to Do

☐ *Thank God for modeling sacrifice so that you can know the true
meaning of "godly leader."*

☐ *Sacrifice something small in your life that benefits you at the expense
of those you lead.*

☐ *Volunteer to do something you would rather not do, but which will
benefit those you lead.*

☐ *Dedicate a sacrificial amount of time to helping others reach critical
goals.*

☐ *Read a book on sacrificial leadership, such as* Servant Leader *by Ken
Blanchard or* Leadership Is an Art *by Max Depree, and apply its
principles to your life.*

Things to Remember

This is love: not that we loved God, but that he loved us and sent his Son as an atoning sacrifice for our sins.

1 John 4:10 NIV

Do as God does. After all, you are his dear children. Let love be your guide. Christ loved us and offered his life for us as a sacrifice that pleases God.

Ephesians 5:1–2 CEV

Now I have it all—and keep getting more! The gifts you sent with Epaphroditus were more than enough, like a sweet-smelling sacrifice roasting on the altar, filling the air with fragrance, pleasing God no end.

Philippians 4:18 THE MESSAGE

You also, as living stones, are being built up a spiritual house, a holy priesthood, to offer up spiritual sacrifices acceptable to God through Jesus Christ.

1 Peter 2:5 NKJV

The generous man will be prosperous, and he who waters will himself be watered.

Proverbs 11:25 NASB

When thou doest alms, let not thy left hand know what thy right hand doeth: That thine alms may be in secret: and thy Father which seeth in secret himself shall reward thee openly.

Matthew 6:3–4 KJV

Great achievement is usually born of great sacrifice, and is never the result of selfishness.

—Napoleon Hill

If one has not given everything, one has given nothing.

—Georges Goynemer

Identity

Who Are You?

You are a chosen generation, a royal priesthood, a holy nation, His own special people, that you may proclaim the praises of Him who called you out of darkness into His marvelous light.

—1 PETER 2:9 NKJV

For fifteen years, James had guided the editorial staff and the direction of a regional travel magazine with a commitment that earned widespread praise and admiration. A tireless promoter, he traveled extensively on a mission to make *Southern Byways* a household name, sacrificing weekends, vacations, and family time. Once, when he was offered a position at a competing magazine, he never even considered leaving. His name had become synonymous with "his" publication, and he couldn't imagine separating himself from it.

But then the bottom fell out. A national publishing conglomerate bought out the magazine's parent company. With another Southern travel magazine already in its stable, the new owners decided to merge the two—making James's position as editor redundant. No problem, everyone told him; he'd land on his feet. And he probably would have. Instead, James sank into a depression so deep that it nearly cost him his family and his future.

In recent years, Pastor Glenn had seen little of James, whose excuses were always the same: he was away at a travel conference or speaking to a group in another state or holed up all weekend working on strategies that would shine the spotlight on *Southern Byways*. As he had long suspected, James's problem stemmed from his close and unhealthy identification with a now defunct magazine. Now, as a physician dealt with James's medical needs, Pastor Glenn dealt with his spiritual needs: primarily, the need to see himself for what he truly was and always would be—a child of God. He knew healing would come only when James started defining himself by his standing in Christ, now and in eternity.

Like James, you are much more than a position you hold in life—or even the sum of the many roles, such as spouse, parent, manager, youth leader, friend, and Christian. That last position, however, is the only unchanging one. It's the one that truly defines you. Your life in Christ is the umbrella under which all those other roles—your temporal, earthly roles—fall into place.

As a child of God, your identity is an eternal one, not one that can be altered by changing life circumstances. In your relationship to Him, you have the security of knowing that no outside force—no downturn in the economy, no change in an organization's direction, no estrangement from friends or family—can separate you from your identity as a member of God's family. Cling to that identity. You may not always hold a leadership position. But you can always hold on to the truth that who you really are is who you are in Christ.

I Will

Learn to think of myself first as a child of God.   *yes*   *no*

Look at my other roles in life in terms of my
relationship to Christ.   *yes*   *no*

Embrace the security of knowing my most
important identity is an eternal one.   *yes*   *no*

Keep a close watch on the significance I attach to
my temporal roles in life.   *yes*   *no*

Realize that emotional health is closely tied to a
healthy identity.   *yes*   *no*

Find my fulfillment in God.   *yes*   *no*

Encourage others to find their identity in Christ.   *yes*   *no*

Things to Do

☐ *Visualize your eternal identity in Christ as an umbrella over your
earthly roles; if necessary, draw a picture or diagram to help you
remember this important image.*

☐ *List every earthly position you hold, including family roles. Ask God to
help you keep each of those roles in the proper perspective.*

☐ *Read the quote from A. W. Tozer and consider how your life would
change if you saw yourself on the receiving end of all that God is.*

☐ *Read several New Testament passages about who you are in Christ,
such as Romans 6:1–18 and the entire book of Ephesians.*

☐ *Start an "I am" list: I am . . . "a new creation" (2 Corinthians 5:17
NKJV); "a royal priest" (1 Peter 2:9). Add to it each time you find a
new biblical definition of who you are in Christ.*

Things to Remember

Now we see in a mirror dimly, but then face to face; now I know in part, but then I will know fully just as I also have been fully known.

1 CORINTHIANS 13:12 NASB

If anyone belongs to Christ, there is a new creation. The old things have gone; everything is made new!

2 CORINTHIANS 5:17 NCV

It is better to trust the LORD than to put confidence in people.

PSALM 118:8 NLT

[Jesus said:] "You did not choose me; I chose you and appointed you to go and bear much fruit, the kind of fruit that endures. And so the Father will give you whatever you ask of him in my name."

JOHN 15:16 GNT

It's in Christ that we find out who we are and what we are living for. Long before we first heard of Christ and got our hopes up, he had his eye on us, had designs on us for glorious living,

EPHESIANS 1:11 THE MESSAGE

You must put on the new self, which is created in God's likeness and reveals itself in the true life that is upright and holy.

EPHESIANS 4:24 GNT

> **To become Christlike is the only thing in the whole world worth caring for, the thing before which every ambition of man is folly and all lower achievement vain.**
>
> **—HENRY DRUMMOND**

> **An infinite God can give all of Himself to each of His children. He does not distribute Himself that each may have a part, but to each one He gives all of Himself as fully as if there were no others.**
>
> **—A. W. TOZER**

Finances

The Bottom Line

The love of money is a root of all kinds of evil, for which some have strayed from the faith in their greediness, and pierced themselves through with many sorrows.

1 TIMOTHY 6:10 NKJV

The biblical story of Gideon—once he became convinced that the call on his life was genuinely from the Lord—is one of fearless and creative leadership. He was the judge of Israel who reduced an army of twenty-two thousand soldiers to a special team of three hundred men armed with trumpets, torches, and empty pitchers, who created panic and confusion among the Midianite enemy forces. Further conflict with the Midianites resulted in Gideon's uncontested victory—and a significant bounty of gold, from which Gideon created a sacred object to commemorate the win. People came from miles around to see this golden ephod—and ended up worshiping the object rather than the Lord, who had given the victory.

Gideon's failing was in taking the resources he had been blessed with and using them for a purpose that became a spiritual snare for the Israelites. The wealth he received became an end in itself, melted down and fashioned into an idol. Today, that sacred object would be called the Israelites' "bottom line." Though it appeared at first to signify a profitable win for the nation, it proved in the end to represent a regrettable loss.

Whether you're dealing with personal, business, or organizational finances, the bottom line for you as a Christian needs to signify something much greater than a dollars-and-cents figure. Shift your thinking away from the figure on the bottom line of a financial statement and toward the end result you want to achieve—the aim of your mission in your life and in your other areas of responsibility. That desired result becomes your new bottom line, and the money and resources you control become a means toward that end.

Consider your sphere of leadership. Are you using finances—and other resources, if you lead a group not dependent on money, such as a Bible study—in the best way possible to accomplish the mission you and your team have defined? Leaders often fall prey to the temptation to embark on resource-draining projects that look impressive but do little to move the organization toward its ultimate goal—or, as Gideon discovered, projects that do more harm than good. Make sure your team is using its resources for the good.

Even if yours is a secular organization, you as a Christian are accountable to God for all that has been entrusted to you. Learn to see money as a means to an end. And keep your eyes on the bottom line that matters, the mission that drives your group's purpose.

I Will

See money as a means to an end rather than an end in itself.   yes ____   no ____

Keep my focus on the results I want to achieve.   yes ____   no ____

Realize that a financial profit can prove to be a loss if not handled properly.   yes ____   no ____

Be accountable to God for the use of all the resources He has given me.   yes ____   no ____

Learn to think of the bottom line in terms of mission rather than money.   yes ____   no ____

Ask God for direction in the wise use of money and other resources.   yes ____   no ____

Things to Do

☐ Read the story of Gideon and the golden ephod in Judges 8:22–28 and come up with a better use for the plunder he received.

☐ Define the "bottom line" for different areas of your life: family, work, ministry or church life, and so forth. Determine how you could use finances or other resource to achieve the results you want.

☐ Seek input from your team on the way resources are being used, specifically asking for suggestions on how they could be better used.

☐ Come up with a strategy for periodically monitoring your group's movement toward its bottom-line purpose.

☐ By some estimations, there are more than twenty-three hundred Bible verses that mention money and possessions. Find ten that are meaningful to you and memorize them.

Things to Remember

Each Sunday each of you must put aside part of what you have earned. If you do this, you won't have to take up a collection when I come.

1 CORINTHIANS 16:2 CEV

[Jesus] said to them, "Take heed and beware of covetousness, for one's life does not consist in the abundance of the things he possesses."

LUKE 12:15 NKJV

"Bring the whole tithe into the storehouse, so that there may be food in My house, and test Me now in this," says the LORD of hosts, "if I will not open for you the windows of heaven and pour out for you a blessing until it overflows."

MALACHI 3:10 NASB

Honor GOD with everything you own; give him the first and the best.

PROVERBS 3:9 THE MESSAGE

[Jesus said:] "Where your treasure is, there your heart will be also."

MATTHEW 6:21 NIV

Jesus said to him, "If you want to be perfect, sell what you own. Give the money to the poor, and you will have treasure in heaven. Then follow me!"

MATTHEW 19:21 GOD'S WORD

Preoccupation with money is the great test of small natures, but only a small test of great ones.

—SEBASTIEN-ROCH NICOLAS DE CHAMFORT

If you make money your god, it will plague you like the devil.

—HENRY FIELDING

Listening

The Key to Connection

My beloved brethren, let every man be swift to hear, slow to speak, slow to wrath.

—James 1:19 NKJV

In the three years Sheryl was in charge of the nursery during church services, the number of babies and toddlers nearly doubled while the number of available volunteer workers increased only slightly. Everyone felt stretched to the limit. Some volunteers quit. Others, like Sheryl, had not attended a service in months. How could they, with so many babies to watch and so few people to watch them?

Soon enough, the parents began to express their concerns about the chaos in the nursery. Some talked to Sheryl in person, some talked to the workers, and others talked among themselves. Feeling that they had not connected in a meaningful way with her, one group of parents enlisted a willing mother to go to the pastor, who in turn talked to Sheryl. All the nursery workers were doing their best, she tried to assure him, despite the unsatisfactory worker-to-child ratio. "So what you need is more volunteers, right?" he asked. "Yes, but we've asked and no one has come forward," she answered. He pressed further: "Sheryl, you need more volunteers. What do you think you need to do to let people know how critical the need is?" "Well, I've told them, but . . ." And so the conversation went, until her frustrated pastor spelled out for her several obvious solutions, including the most drastic: eliminating the nursery entirely.

Panicked, Sheryl scrambled to come up with a better idea. She prayed. She begged for help. She just *couldn't* close the nursery; she'd have to manage somehow. But soon, it was the babies themselves who were raising the biggest outcry. One Sunday morning, the noise coming from a roomful of very unhappy children reached the sanctuary. That week, the word went out: The nursery was closed until more volunteers came forward to help out with the overload.

Toward the end of the week, Sheryl met with her pastor. "Why did it have to come to this?" she asked. "Why couldn't God have intervened and done something?" "He did," Pastor Bill said. "Several times. Actually, He's been speaking to you about this for months." "Well, I prayed, but He never told me what to do," she said. Patiently, Pastor Bill listed the number of ways and the number of people God "spoke" through: the parents, the workers, the children, the circumstances, even Pastor Bill himself. The problem, as Sheryl slowly realized, was her inability to listen carefully and respond thoughtfully.

That day, Sheryl began to learn what it meant to truly listen, both with her ears and with her heart. As Pastor Bill explained, it's not enough to mechanically process the sounds that enter your ear; you also have to learn to "hear" a person's intention or anguish or a multitude of things that were left unsaid. Effective leaders, he pointed, learn to listen with their ears and their hearts—because when leaders listen with that kind of attentiveness, the people around them feel valued and more comfortable in sharing their concerns. Leaders especially need to listen to critics, he said, because no matter how misguided they seem to be, there may be just a kernel of truth in their criticism. Above all, a leader needs to hear what God might be saying through both critics and supporters alike.

As Pat Williams, senior vice president of the Orlando Magic basketball team, has pointed out, no leader has ever been criticized for listening too much. It's one of the paradoxes he writes about in *The Paradox of Power: A Transforming View of Leadership*. He advises leaders to ask intelligent questions in order to get people to open up and offer suggestions, and to make it their goal to learn from whatever is said to them.

As Williams also points out, listening was an important element of Jesus' leadership style: He *listened* to what the people said to Him. And He continues to listen today, as you express your concerns and ask for His guidance and seek His help in solving those pressing problems that keep nagging at you. Remember that He often speaks through other people and through circumstances. As you're praying about difficult situations, be attentive to all that is being said and all that is happening around you. That's where you are likely to find your solutions.

I Will

Learn to listen with my ears and my heart.   yes ___ no ___

Be attentive to all that is said and done around me.   yes ___ no ___

Realize that God speaks to me through people and
circumstances.   yes ___ no ___

Follow Jesus' example by listening to my followers.   yes ___ no ___

Understand that people feel valued when I truly
listen to them.   yes ___ no ___

Ask thoughtful questions to encourage others to
express themselves.   yes ___ no ___

Things to Do

☐ *Read about Jesus' interaction with Nicodemus, a cautious Pharisee yet one who felt comfortable questioning Jesus, in John 3:1–21.*

☐ *Make it a point to spend some relaxed time with your group this week. Simply listen and observe, and see how much you learn.*

☐ *Express to your team your openness in listening to them regarding problems and solutions—even if the group you lead consists of toddlers. They can come up with some great ideas!*

☐ *Observe the body language (eye contact, for example) of someone who seems to genuinely listen to you and practice learning the same "language."*

☐ *List the various ways God can speak to you (people, events, the Bible, prayer, and so forth). At the end of this week, check off all the ways He "did" speak to you.*

Things to Remember

[God said:] "If my people would but listen to me, if Israel would follow my ways, how quickly would I subdue their enemies and turn my hand against their foes!"

PSALM 81:13–14 NIV

This is what the LORD says—your Redeemer, the Holy One of Israel: "I am the LORD your God, who teaches you what is best for you, who directs you in the way you should go."

ISAIAH 48:17 NIV

[Jesus said:] "The gatekeeper opens the gate for him, and the sheep hear his voice and come to him. He calls his own sheep by name and leads them out."

John 10:3 NLT

The LORD will continually guide you and satisfy you even in sun-baked places. He will strengthen your bones. You will become like a watered garden and like a spring whose water does not stop flowing.

ISAIAH 58:11 GOD'S WORD

One who looks intently at the perfect law, the law of liberty, and abides by it, not having become a forgetful hearer but an effectual doer, this man will be blessed in what he does.

JAMES 1:25 NASB

[Jesus said:] "My sheep hear My voice, and I know them, and they follow Me."

JOHN 10:27 NKJV

[Jesus said:] "When, however, the Spirit comes, who reveals the truth about God, he will lead you into all the truth. He will not speak on his own authority, but he will speak of what he hears and will tell you of things to come."

JOHN 16:13 GNT

Come, my children, listen to me; I will teach you the fear of the LORD.

PSALM 34:11 NIV

Then Jesus said, "You people who can hear me, listen!"

MARK 4:9 NCV

God says, "My people, listen to me; Israel, I will testify against you. I am God, your God."

PSALM 50:7 NCV

[David wrote:] As I lie on my bed, I remember you. Through the long hours of the night, I think about you.

PSALM 63:6 GOD'S WORD

"If you have ears, then, listen to what the Spirit says to the churches!"

REVELATION 2:29 GNT

The greatest gift you can give another is the purity of your attention.

—RICHARD MOSS

Learn to listen. Opportunity could be knocking at your door very softly.

—FRANK TYGER

Planning

Charting the Course

I know the thoughts that I think toward you, says the
LORD, thoughts of peace and not of evil, to give you a
future and a hope.

—JEREMIAH 29:11 NKJV

As a royal cupbearer, Nehemiah held a position of honor
in the court of the king of Babylon. First and foremost, though,
he was a Jew, and when he heard of the ruinous condition of
Jerusalem from which most Jews had been exiled, he grieved—
for a while. Then, it was time for action, and that required a
plan. First, he obtained the king's favor to rebuild the walls of
the city, along with letters of approval to present to local
officials, instructions to those in authority to provide
Nehemiah with the materials he needed, and an armed escort
to accompany him from the Babylonian capital of Susa to
Jerusalem, a distance of nearly a thousand miles.

Once there, Nehemiah surveyed the damage, enlisted
workers, acquired the needed resources, appointed leaders,
divided up tasks among them, and then rolled up his sleeves
and got to work. His focused commitment to the task at hand,
often in the face of ridicule and torment from one local
official, provides an exemplary model of leadership at its best.
His mission, stirred as it was from a passionate desire to see

the city of his ancestors rebuilt, did not blind him to the need for a well-thought-out plan.

Leadership experts place a high value on wise planning. They often use the image of a road map in training others to develop an effective plan for their organization as a whole as well as individual projects. It's a good image to keep in mind, because a road map not only shows your destination but also the stopping points along the way and a means of measuring your progress. And just as a road trip can be broken up into smaller "legs," both long-range and short-term plans can be broken up into smaller, more manageable—and less daunting—segments.

Experts also recognize one of the pitfalls of the planning process: spending too much time *planning* and not enough time *doing*. "A good plan today is better than a perfect plan tomorrow," said General George S. Patton, well aware of the potential risks in delay. Wise leaders know to bring others into the planning process—especially God, seeking His wisdom and direction and thereby reducing the risk of error. In implementing the resulting plan, they also realize the need for flexibility and continued dependence on God should a change in direction be required.

Plan for the future with God's help. Break larger projects into doable tasks. Measure your progress along the way. And remember to keep your plans flexible, as circumstances change and as God redirects.

I Will

Recognize the importance of planning.
<u>yes</u>　　<u>no</u>

Develop a means of measuring progress as a plan is
implemented.
<u>yes</u>　　<u>no</u>

Seek God's guidance and direction in the planning
process.
<u>yes</u>　　<u>no</u>

Resist the temptation to overplan.
<u>yes</u>　　<u>no</u>

Keep my plans flexible and open to change, as God
directs or circumstances dictate.
<u>yes</u>　　<u>no</u>

Bring other people into the planning process.
<u>yes</u>　　<u>no</u>

Things to Do

☐ Take a current or upcoming project and review it in light of what you
have read about planning in this devotional.

☐ Memorize Luke 14:28–30.

☐ Think back to a project in which a bit more planning might have
produced a better outcome.

☐ Read the book of Nehemiah and take note of his leadership style.

☐ Create a method for allowing others in your group to be a part of the
planning process.

☐ Read James 4:13–16 to see what it has to say about making plans
apart from God's direction.

☐ Ask God in which area of your life or work you need to make
long-range plans.

Things to Remember

[Jesus said:] "If one of you is planning to build a tower, you sit down first and figure out what it will cost, to see if you have enough money to finish the job. If you don't, you will not be able to finish the tower after laying the foundation; and all who see what happened will make fun of you. 'You began to build but can't finish the job!' they will say."

LUKE 14:28–30 GNT

[Jesus said:] "I'm no longer calling you servants because servants don't understand what their master is thinking and planning. No, I've named you friends because I've let you in on everything I've heard from the Father."

JOHN 15:15 THE MESSAGE

Who ever knows what you're thinking and planning except you yourself? The same with God—except that he not only knows what he's thinking, but he lets us in on it. God offers a full report on the gifts of life and salvation that he is giving us.

1 CORINTHIANS 2:11–12 THE MESSAGE

Long, long ago he decided to adopt us into his family through Jesus Christ. (What pleasure he took in planning this!)

EPHESIANS 1:5 THE MESSAGE

Planning is bringing the future into the present so that you can do something about it now.

—ALAN LAKEIN

Whatever failures I have known, whatever errors I have committed, whatever follies I have witnessed in private and public life have been the consequence of action without thought.

—BERNARD M. BARUCH

Failure

Your Best Friend

*If our heart condemns us, God is greater than our heart,
and knows all things.*

—1 JOHN 3:20 NKJV

Thomas Edison, Louisa May Alcott, Michael Jordan, Walt
Disney, Ludwig von Beethoven, Albert Einstein, Theodore
Geisel (better known as Dr. Seuss). What each of those famous
and talented people have in common is that at some point in
their lives, someone considered them to be a failure. People
said Edison and Einstein weren't smart enough; Alcott and
Geisel couldn't write; Jordan couldn't play basketball;
Beethoven couldn't compose; and Disney lacked imagination.
What set these famous "failures" apart—aside from their
accomplishments—was their ability to rise above the gloomy
predictions and bounce back from their failures stronger than
ever.

Throughout his life, Henry Ford, who suffered numerous
setbacks including bankruptcies, maintained that failure
proved to be the best teacher he ever had. Other leaders have
called failure a friend, a springboard or a stepping stone to
success, a temporary change in direction—even the fertilizer in
which healthy growth can occur. They point to the fear of
failure as one of the greatest obstacles to innovation, because a

leader afraid to fail is a leader afraid to take the kind of risk necessary for creative change to occur.

Fear of failure paralyzes even those who believe in God's power and His interaction in their lives. The memories of past failures cause them to think that God cannot trust them with greater responsibility, and their ministry stagnates. If that describes you, consider the life of Peter. Brash, impetuous, and cowardly, the disciple who denied that he ever knew Jesus became the post-Resurrection leader of the followers of Christ in Jerusalem. Jesus Himself entrusted the care of His followers into the hands of this first century "failure." God trusted him with greater responsibility than any of his friends would have thought possible back when he was known as just another fisherman.

If you've experienced failure, even one that was highly public and humiliating, admit your mistake and allow God to use it to transform you into the leader He wants you to be. If you're so afraid of failure that you've stopped taking risks and your organization has stopped moving forward, give that fear to God and trust Him to help you make wise decisions to get things moving again. Stop believing those people who predict failure for you—especially if one of those people is you. What matters is what God believes about you, and He has not given up on you. Even better, He never will.

I Will

Openly admit my mistakes.

*yes*____ *no*____

Learn from my failures.

*yes*____ *no*____

Trust God to help me bounce back when I fail.

*yes*____ *no*____

Realize that risking failure is essential to making innovative changes.

*yes*____ *no*____

Give my fear of failure to God.

*yes*____ *no*____

Refuse to believe anyone who unjustifiably questions my ability to lead.

*yes*____ *no*____

Believe God can transform me into the person and the leader He wants me to be.

*yes*____ *no*____

Things to Do

☐ Choose a "famous failure," such as Thomas Edison, and read about his or her experiences with failure.

☐ Think about a past failure in your life and ask God to show you what He wants you to learn from the experience.

☐ Make a list of all the risks you would take in your organization if you had no fear of failure; choose at least one to follow through on.

☐ Help a friend or colleague who is plagued by a sense of failure.

☐ Read about Peter in the Gospels and Acts, and how God transformed him from a cowardly liar into a fearless leader.

☐ Look for contemporary examples of people who have failed and emerged stronger (e.g., Donna Rice, who turned public humiliation into an antipornography ministry).

Things to Remember

Not one of all the LORD'S good promises to the house of Israel failed; every one was fulfilled.

JOSHUA 21:45 NIV

The LORD will make you the head, not the tail. You will always be at the top, never at the bottom, if you faithfully obey the commands of the LORD your God that I am giving you today.

DEUTERONOMY 28:13 GOD'S WORD

A good person will never fail; he will always be remembered.

PSALM 112:6 GNT

Let us try as hard as we can to enter God's rest so that no one will fail by following the example of those who refused to obey.

HEBREWS 4:11 NCV

"I will forgive their wrongdoings, and I will never again remember their sins."

HEBREWS 8:12 NLT

Sin shall not have dominion over you, for you are not under law but under grace.

ROMANS 6:14 NKJV

We must expect to fail . . . but fail in a learning posture, determined not to repeat the mistakes, and to maximize the benefits from what is learned in the process.

—TED W. ENGSTROM

Failure is a detour, not a dead-end street.

—ZIG ZIGLAR

Growth

Learning to Multiply

From whom the whole body, joined and knit together by what every joint supplies, according to the effective working by which every part does its share, causes growth of the body for the edifying of itself in love.

—EPHESIANS 4:16 NKJV

When Wesley bought a small printing company, it was one of the few businesses of its kind in the area. Compared to the competition, the services it offered were extensive, and Wesley was determined to see the company grow. With the zeal of a man on a mission, he devised a strategy for growth that was as radical as it was unrealistic. He ordered state-of-the-art equipment, began remodeling the existing facilities, and got the word out about the new ownership and upgraded services. He was soon able to hire two additional employees.

Meanwhile, Wesley's wife tried to remain supportive, but all their assets were now tied up in this new venture, and they were seriously in debt. Cynthia attempted to reason with him, asking him to just slow things down a bit. "We have to grow the business," he would always respond. He was so focused on the growth of his own company that he failed to keep abreast of the local business news—including an item in the newspaper indicating that not one but two big office supply stores featuring comprehensive printing services would be coming to the area within the next year. By the time he found out, it was too late to change course. Not surprisingly, when the stores opened they siphoned off not only many of Wesley's clients but also his most experienced employees. Within another year, his company had gone bankrupt.

Whether you're in business or ministry, it's likely that you've been encouraged to add to the "numbers." In business, that usually means increasing revenue; in ministry, it means drawing more people. And that's generally a good thing; adding to the bottom line or bringing people to Christ often means that you're doing your job and fulfilling your calling. But not all growth is good. "Growth for the sake of growth is the ideology of the cancer cell," as Edward Abbey once said. As Wesley discovered, an unhealthy focus on growth can have disastrous consequences.

Examine your motives in setting a goal for the growth you want to achieve. If you're in business, the consequences of an unhealthy focus on growth include financial ruin. In ministry, the consequences are even heavier if the increased numbers fail to represent lives genuinely changed by God. In both cases, people are devalued; if the leadership sees each person—whether customer or convert—as just another number, each person will begin to feel like just another number. That's not healthy, nor is it the way you want your leadership to be perceived. Growth is good, but only if it stems from a healthy motivation.

I Will

Develop a healthy attitude toward growth.

yes ___ *no* ___

Realize that not all growth is good.

yes ___ *no* ___

Seek God's guidance before making growth-related decisions.

yes ___ *no* ___

Place a higher value on people than on the numbers they represent.

yes ___ *no* ___

Be aware of the consequences of an unhealthy focus on growth.

yes ___ *no* ___

Take circumstances and others' opinions into account when planning for growth.

yes ___ *no* ___

Things to Do

☐ *Assess your organization's current approach to growth.*

☐ *Create short- and long-range growth plans (or revise existing plans) after you've spent time in prayer about it.*

☐ *Start a pro-and-con list relating to growth in your organization (a pro may be "evidence of successful outreach," while a con may be "need larger facilities"). Analyze the results.*

☐ *Read the story of the explosive growth of the early church in Acts 2— and consider the task Peter had as the leader of three thousand new converts all at once.*

☐ *Look at your group's history of growth and determine what accounted for any spikes in growth.*

☐ *Ask your team for ideas on how to make your organization grow in a healthy way.*

Things to Remember

The word of God spread. The number of disciples in Jerusalem increased rapidly, and a large number of priests became obedient to the faith.

ACTS 6:7 NIV

[Paul wrote:] I planted, Apollos watered, but God was causing the growth.

1 CORINTHIANS 3:6 NASB

[Paul wrote:] I plan to be around awhile, companion to you as your growth and joy in this life of trusting God continues.

PHILIPPIANS 1:25 THE MESSAGE

May the LORD, the God of your fathers, increase you a thousand times and bless you as he has promised!

DEUTERONOMY 1:11 NIV

I command you today to love the LORD your God, to walk in his ways, and to keep his commands, decrees and laws; then you will live and increase, and the LORD your God will bless you in the land you are entering to possess.

DEUTERONOMY 30:16 NIV

"I will look on you with favor and make you fruitful and increase your numbers, and I will keep my covenant with you."

LEVITICUS 26:9 NIV

> The fatal metaphor of progress, which means leaving things behind us, has utterly obscured the real idea of growth, which means leaving things inside us.
>
> —G. K. CHESTERTON

> We grow because we struggle, we learn, and we overcome.
>
> —R. C. ALLEN

Teachability

What You Don't Know

For this very reason, giving all diligence, add to your faith virtue, to virtue knowledge.

—2 PETER 1:5 NKJV

As a longtime teacher of the teen Bible class in a large suburban church, Kay had enjoyed the accolades of students and parents alike who credited her with bringing the Bible to life and making its teachings meaningful to twenty-first-century youth. So popular was her class that the time was changed from Sunday morning to late Sunday afternoon to allow teenagers from other churches to attend. Her ability to communicate with the youth on Sunday was only strengthened by her weekday job—Kay was also an English teacher in the local high school.

One night, at a meeting of all the church's ministry leaders and class teachers, Pastor Charlie announced that a class on spiritual gifts for leaders would be starting in two weeks. The idea, he said, was to make sure all of the church's leaders were aware of the spiritual gifts God had given them, such as the gifts of service, prayer, and evangelism, and therefore to make sure that all the leaders were being used to their fullest potential. As an added benefit, once the leaders completed the six-week course they would be in a much better position to present it to others in the church.

Kay balked at the idea. Wasn't it evident that her gift was teaching? Why should she sacrifice two hours of her time each week for six weeks to discover what she already knew? As she sat in the meeting, she devised a strategy for being exempted from the course. A few days later, she sat in Pastor Charlie's office and put her strategy to work, laying out for him her extensive teaching experience and her completion of a spiritual gifts inventory years earlier.

"Well, you realize your participation is not mandatory," her pastor said. "But we would like all the leaders to attend. Other churches that have given this course to their leaders have been amazed at the results—lots of their people discovered new things about themselves, and their ministries expanded as a result." After a few more exchanges, Kay relented, agreeing to her pastor's suggestion that she attend the first two meetings and then decide if she wanted to continue.

What Kay learned in those first two classes made her hungry for more. She learned that she also had the gifts of encouragement and leadership administration, and suddenly realized the multitude of ministry opportunities that had opened up to her. As she stood in the hallway thanking Pastor Charlie at the close of the final session, he smiled warmly and reminded her of her initial resistance. "Once you got past that hurdle," he said, "it turned out that you had a teachable spirit after all." A teachable spirit—Kay liked the sound of that, especially since it applied to her.

A teachable spirit is evidence of a flexible approach to life. Stubborn, rigid people are not teachable. Jesus knew that when He called His disciples; they had an almost childlike curiosity about the things of God. They were eager to learn and eager to understand the difficult things Jesus often said. He knew better than to choose His followers from among, say, the Pharisees, who often acted as if they knew it all. No, He sought the humble, the inquisitive, the seeking—the teachable. That's what He wants in His followers today, an ability to learn from Him and from life and from all the wisdom and knowledge contained in the Bible.

Would the people in your organization describe you as teachable? They would if you frequently acknowledge the insights you've gained and the information you've acquired from a variety of sources—including your followers and people outside your own organization. They would also describe you as teachable if you regularly hang around and ask questions about the work people are doing or about their interests or about their mission in life, depending on the type of group you lead. And they would if you make it a rule to give credit where credit is due, recognizing those people who have taught the entire team, yourself included, valuable lessons.

If you can be described as teachable, then you are the kind of leader Jesus wants His people to have. Learn from God's Spirit; learn from the teachable people whose stories are told in the Bible; learn from those in authority over you—and from those you have authority over.

I Will

Cultivate a teachable spirit. _yes_ _no_

Be flexible in leadership and in life. _yes_ _no_

Realize that my followers have much to teach me. _yes_ _no_

Acknowledge those I have learned from. _yes_ _no_

Develop an inquisitive mind. _yes_ _no_

Realize that learning is a lifelong endeavor. _yes_ _no_

Regularly seek wisdom and knowledge from the Bible. _yes_ _no_

Things to Do

☐ *Begin the habit of reading articles on leadership either on-line or by subscribing to a periodical like Leadership Journal.*

☐ *If you haven't already, begin a systematic study of the Bible.*

☐ *Think of some learning opportunities you've recently dismissed, and resolve to take advantage of others as they arise.*

☐ *Ask your colleagues about training sessions or courses they've found helpful in their work.*

☐ *Choose a subject or skill you've always wanted to master, and take the first step toward mastering it.*

☐ *Give the members of your team an opportunity to teach others, including you, about their responsibilities (or their interests, for children).*

Things to Remember

Start with GOD—the first step in learning is bowing down to GOD; only fools thumb their noses at such wisdom and learning.

PROVERBS 1:7 THE MESSAGE

Let the wise listen and add to their learning, and let the discerning get guidance.

PROVERBS 1:5 NIV

Truth, wisdom, learning, and good sense— these are worth payng for, but too valuable for you to sell.

PROVERBS 23:23 GNT

Wise men and women are always learning, always listening for fresh insights.

PROVERBS 18:15 THE MESSAGE

Give instruction to the wise, and they will become wiser still; teach the righteous and they will gain in learning.

PROVERBS 9:9 NRSV

If you stop learning, you will forget what you already know.

PROVERBS 19:27 CEV

They spent their time in learning from the apostles, taking part in the fellowship, and sharing in the fellowship meals and the prayers.

ACTS 2:42 GNT

[Jesus said:] "This is what the prophets meant when they wrote, 'And then they will all be personally taught by God.' Anyone who has spent any time at all listening to the Father, really listening and therefore learning, comes to me to be taught personally—to see it with his own eyes, hear it with his own ears, from me, since I have it firsthand from the Father."

JOHN 6:45 THE MESSAGE

I pray that God will be kind to you and will let you live in perfect peace! May you keep learning more and more about God and our Lord Jesus.

2 PETER 1:2 CEV

The wise in heart will be called prudent, and sweetness of the lips increases learning.

PROVERBS 16:21 NKJV

The heart of the wise teaches his mouth, and adds learning to his lips.

PROVERBS 16:23 NKJV

Yes, beg for knowledge; plead for insight. Look for it as hard as you would for silver or some hidden treasure. If you do, you will know what it means to fear the LORD and you will succeed in learning about God.

PROVERBS 2:3–5 GNT

Learning is not compulsory, but neither is survival.

—W. EDWARDS DEMING

It's what you learn after you know it all that counts.

—JOHN WOODEN

Facing the Truth

Clear As Day

[Jesus said:] "And you shall know the truth, and the truth shall make you free."

—JOHN 8:32 NKJV

Week after week, the news coming from corporate headquarters was positive. The company was in sound financial shape, experiencing exponential growth and enjoying the favor of several powerful members of Congress. The company had even won awards for the strides it was making toward environmental responsibility. But suddenly, everything bottomed out. Overnight, Enron went from being a major player in the energy-trading industry to a classic example of greed, mismanagement, and the ultimate failure of the positive spin.

Enron employees—and their counterparts in other scandal-decimated companies—were left to face the truth: Not only had they been lied to for years but they had also lost everything they had invested in the company—their 401(k) retirement funds, their livelihood, and their trust. Also left to face the truth was the corporate leadership, everyone from those in the upper echelon, who also face prison sentences, to the junior executives and departmental managers, whose credibility and trustworthiness has been eroded, whether justifiably or not.

The lessons to be learned from the Enron debacle are many, but one of the foundational lessons is that which relates to truth. The truth was, Enron had been playing fast and loose for years and had gotten by with it. Directors looked the other way. Government agencies looked the other way. Executives looked the other way. No one seemed willing to face the truth. The words of Jesus in John 8:32, as well known as they are, just did not sink in.

The cost of looking the other way, of putting a positive spin on a potentially damaging situation, is a high one. And as many a leader has discovered too late, the top person is all too often the last to get the bad news but the first to be called to account for it. Wise leaders find protection from that kind of disaster by surrounding themselves with people who will give it to them straight, people who know that the ugly truth is far better than a beautiful lie. They know they must keep in close contact with the people in their group, asking the right questions and observing the work that's being done and fixing problems as they go.

Be up front with people about the reality of the condition your group is in. You're likely to find them more than willing to pitch in and help get your organization out of a potential mess. People appreciate honesty, and their opinion of you will likely be raised a notch or two as they witness your willingness to confront the truth.

I Will

Strive to fearlessly face reality.

yes   *no*

Choose close associates who know they must
always tell me the truth.

yes   *no*

Keep my team informed about potential problems.

yes   *no*

Maintain close contact with people in my
organization.

yes   *no*

Fix problems as they arise.

yes   *no*

Recognize the high cost of the positive spin.

yes   *no*

Be observant.

yes   *no*

Things to Do

☐ *The Bible tells it straight; read Acts 15:36–41, in which the writer
describes an unpleasant incident rather than putting a positive spin
on it.*

☐ *Memorize John 8:32 and make it a motto for your role as a leader.*

☐ *Clarify to the members of your team your need for honest,
forthright reports.*

☐ *Share any negative information you've been withholding from your
group, if you determine it's something they need to know.*

☐ *Read an article or two on one of the recent corporate scandals to see
how the inability to face reality figured in the company's downfall.*

☐ *Ask God to show you any areas of responsibility in which you are
vulnerable to believing a beautiful lie rather than the ugly truth.*

Things to Remember

[Jesus said:] "You pretender! First take the piece of wood out of your own eye. Then you will be able to see clearly to take the bit of sawdust out of your friend's eye."

MATTHEW 7:5 NIrV

Abruptly Jesus broke into prayer: "Thank you, Father, Lord of heaven and earth. You've concealed your ways from sophisticates and know-it-alls, but spelled them out clearly to ordinary people."

MATTHEW 11:25 THE MESSAGE

[Paul wrote:] I can do anything I want to if Christ has not said no, but some of these things aren't good for me. Even if I am allowed to do them, I'll refuse to if I think they might get such a grip on me that I can't stop easily when I want to.

1 CORINTHIANS 6:12 TLB

Christ has freed us so that we may enjoy the benefits of freedom. Therefore, be firm [in this freedom], and don't become slaves again.

GALATIANS 5:1 GOD'S WORD

I have chosen to be faithful; I have determined to live by your laws.

PSALM 119:30 NLT

> **You never find yourself until you face the truth.**
>
> —PEARL BAILEY

> **Life's experiences are intended to make you eventually face yourself. Face reality!**
>
> —HAROLD SHERMAN

Procrastination

Ahead of the Curve

Therefore we also, since we are surrounded by so great a cloud of witnesses, let us lay aside every weight, and the sin which so easily ensnares us, and let us run with endurance the race that is set before us.

—HEBREWS 12:1 NKJV

Margaret stared at the computer screen as another article on Colonial Williamsburg loaded. This one included a link to information on handicapped access, exactly what she needed. She decided she should read the entire article first—you never know what you might learn. She read to the end, clicked on the handicapped access link, and discovered more links to items of interest to senior citizens in the Williamsburg area. Well, she couldn't let those go without checking them out. What kind of seniors' housing administrator would she be if she didn't investigate all the possibilities for the residents' upcoming trip?

She knew the answer to that—she'd be a *better* administrator. Planning the trip was not even her responsibility; Ruth, the facilities' highly capable activities director, handled all the travel and sightseeing arrangements. She also knew why she was spending her time checking out Williamsburg: The annual budget was due. As long as she could convince herself that she had more pressing concerns, she could put off working on the dreaded budget. Despite a rapidly approaching deadline, more than one reminder from the board of directors, and repeated nudgings from the Holy Spirit, Margaret always seemed to find something more important to do.

You probably know some of the alternatives she ended up with: risk her health with a series of coffee-laced all-nighters, throw together an unsatisfactory document at the last minute, miss the deadline altogether. All stressful solutions, none of them acceptable. And not the kind of example Margaret wanted to set for the rest of the staff.

Putting off unpleasant tasks only makes them more unpleasant, as Margaret learned. But putting off any task, even those that you're not dreading, can be stressful as they nag at you and distract you until you finally relent and get them done. You can reduce that potential stress by following the common-sense advice of time management experts: Do unpleasant tasks first. Chip away at big projects by doing a little at a time. Set a time limit on jobs you dislike and stick to it. Make an appointment with yourself to do routine paperwork. Avoid negative self-talk ("I dread doing that budget!").

Only you—and God—know why you procrastinate. Get to the heart of that, and you can better handle those tasks you keep putting off. Take a deep breath, utter a quiet prayer, and get to work. You know you'll feel better when it's done. And when you are done, make a resolution to eliminate procrastination from your routine. Don't put it off.

I Will

Take care of things in a timely manner.   yes _____ no _____

Respond immediately to the promptings of God's
Spirit.   yes _____ no _____

Recognize the subtle methods and weak excuses I
use when I procrastinate.   yes _____ no _____

Avoid putting off distasteful tasks.   yes _____ no _____

Be aware of the stress that results when I put
things off.   yes _____ no _____

Be an example of responsible leadership.   yes _____ no _____

Things to Do

☐ Tackle that one chore you've been putting off for too long.

☐ Develop a system for prioritizing routine tasks.

☐ Set a realistic deadline to complete an upcoming project and resolve to
   stick to it.

☐ Make an appointment to spend time with God, seeking His direction for
   your schedule.

☐ Meet with other members of your team and develop a means of keeping
   each other accountable for fulfilling responsibilities on time.

☐ Apologize to anyone whose job may have been made more difficult by
   your procrastination.

☐ Post a yearly calendar with clearly marked deadlines for annual,
   monthly, and weekly tasks.

Things to Remember

Do not withhold good from those to whom it is due, when it is in the power of your hand to do so.

PROVERBS 3:27 NKJV

When you make a vow to God, do not delay fulfilling it; for he has no pleasure in fools. Fulfill what you vow.

ECCLESIASTES 5:4 NRSV

We desire that each one of you show the same diligence to the full assurance of hope until the end.

HEBREWS 6:11 NKJV

[The psalmist wrote:] I will hurry, without lingering, to obey your commands.

PSALM 119:60 NLT

Don't tell your neighbor, "Maybe some other time," or, "Try me tomorrow," when the money's right there in your pocket.

PROVERBS 3:28 THE MESSAGE

[Jesus said:] "Listen carefully. I'm speaking sober truth to you. I speak only of what I know by experience; I give witness only to what I have seen with my own eyes. There is nothing secondhand here, no hearsay. Yet instead of facing the evidence and accepting it, you procrastinate with questions."

JOHN 3:11 THE MESSAGE

If you want to make an easy job seem mighty hard, just keep putting off doing it.

—OLIN MILLER

The greatest amount of wasted time is the time not getting started.

—DAWSON TROTMAN

Role Modeling

Pass It On

Imitate me, just as I also imitate Christ.

—1 Corinthians 11:1 NKJV

If you're a leader, you're a role model. That's a fact you cannot change. What you can change is the kind of role model you are, and for instruction on how to do that, there's no better manual than your Bible. Jesus, the greatest role model who ever lived, not only left His advice on how to live an exemplary life but also modeled an exemplary life during His brief time on earth.

Leaders in particular can learn a lot from Jesus. Following His style of leadership will ensure that you maintain the right attitude, balance the many demands on you and on your time, and create a lasting impression on those who choose you as their earthly role model. His leadership style was characterized by an unwavering commitment to the Father who sent Him and the people He was sent to serve.

Jesus loved. That's the essence of Jesus' effectiveness as a leader. He loved the Father. He loved the people He ministered to, and He treated His followers with compassion and tenderness. His death on the cross was the ultimate act of love on their behalf.

Jesus taught. He took advantage of every teaching opportunity that arose. At those times when He had to rebuke a disciple or two, He did so as a teacher. He wanted them to learn from Him and to learn well, because He knew His time with them was short.

Jesus delegated. He chose twelve men to travel with Him and gave them authority to act in His name. He trained them to be able to pick up the work when He was no longer there to do it for them. He created a fellowship of believers, which in turn served as a role model for the early church.

Jesus befriended. Apart from the twelve disciples, Jesus also had friends, most notably Lazarus, Mary, and Martha, at whose home in Bethany He appears to have been a fairly regular guest. He attended dinner parties and other events at which He was able to relax from the pressures of ministry.

Jesus accepted. He accepted everyone. He reached out to the untouchables, the lepers, just as readily as He reached out to people in very other stratum of society—including any Pharisee, like Nicodemus, who was willing to humble himself and seek Jesus' help.

Jesus withdrew. He understood the stresses and demands of leadership and spent time away from the crowds so He could rest and be refreshed. He knew that rest was essential to living a balanced life.

Jesus prayed. Not only did He teach others how to pray, He modeled prayer for them. The hours He spent apart from His disciples, often in the middle of the night, were hours spent in prayer. His desire to spend time with the Father continues to serve as an example to His followers today.

Jesus trusted. His unshakeable trust in the Father was evident to all who came in contact with Him. And His confidence in the Father's will was never more evident than in the Garden of Gethsemane the night before His crucifixion.

Jesus obeyed. Although He was God Himself, Jesus spent His time on earth doing the will of the Father. He was obedient, as the Bible points out, to the point of death—death on the cross.

That's a tough act to follow, for sure. But Jesus never modeled any behavior that His followers could not emulate—including walking on water. Look at what He modeled: love, teaching, delegation, friendship, acceptance, rest, prayer, trust, obedience, all behaviors and activities that you can adopt for yourself and most likely already have.

Jesus did not come to earth to be an example of the kind of person, the kind of leader, you could never become. The very act of living on earth as a flesh-and-blood man provides ample proof that He was, in His humanity, just like you. And when He left earth, the Father sent His Spirit to empower you to live the kind of life Jesus lived. Your responsibility in this is not to live a perfect life but to learn from Jesus' example and draw on the power of God's Spirit to follow that example. You have the opportunity to emulate the best. You'll never find a better role model.

I Will

Realize that as a leader I am already a role model.   *yes*   *no*

Learn from Jesus' example.   *yes*   *no*

Draw on the power of God's Spirit to live a godly life.   *yes*   *no*

Understand that God does not expect me to live a perfect life.   *yes*   *no*

Believe that by emulating Jesus, I can become a better leader and positive role model.   *yes*   *no*

Appreciate the truth of Jesus' humanity.   *yes*   *no*

Be grateful for the empowerment of the Holy Spirit.   *yes*   *no*

Things to Do

☐ *Determine who your role models are and list the qualities that you admire in them.*

☐ *Examine the character of the ultimate role model—Jesus—and resolve to emulate Him.*

☐ *Ask two or three colleagues (independent of each other) to rate your assets as a role model.*

☐ *Remind yourself throughout the day tomorrow that you are most likely someone's role model. See how that changes your behavior.*

☐ *Create a set of goals for becoming a better role model.*

☐ *Complete these sentences with the same phrase based on your desire for your group: "I want others to _____. Therefore I must _____." (Examples: be on time, meet deadlines, be courteous.)*

Things to Remember

We do not want you to become lazy, but to be like those who believe and are patient, and so receive what God has promised.

HEBREWS 6:12 GNT

You received the message with joy from the Holy Spirit in spite of the severe suffering it brought you. In this way, you imitated both us and the Lord. As a result, you yourselves became an example to all the Christians in Greece.

1 THESSALONIANS 1:6–7 NLT

My life is an example to many, because you have been my strength and protection.
Psalm 71:7 NLT

[Paul wrote:] You stare and stare at the obvious, but you can't see the forest for the trees. If you're looking for a clear example of someone on Christ's side, why do you so quickly cut me out? Believe me, I am quite sure of my standing with Christ.

2 CORINTHIANS 10:7 THE MESSAGE

He did what was pleasing in the LORD's sight and followed the example of his ancestor David. He did not turn aside from doing what was right.

2 KINGS 22:2 NLT

[Jesus said:] "I have given you an example to follow. Do as I have done to you."

JOHN 13:15 NLT

[Paul wrote:] Now, dear brothers and sisters, we give you this command with the authority of our Lord Jesus Christ: Stay away from any Christian who lives in idleness and doesn't follow the tradition of hard work we gave you. For you know that you ought to follow our example. We were never lazy when we were with you.

2 THESSALONIANS 3:6–7 NLT

"Our father is Abraham," they declared. "No," Jesus replied, "for if you were children of Abraham, you would follow his good example."

JOHN 8:39 NLT

Ezekiel will be your example. The way he did it is the way you'll do it. "When this happens you'll recognize that I am GOD, the Master."

EZEKIEL 24:24 THE MESSAGE

[Paul wrote:] I am a free man. I am an apostle. I have seen Jesus our Lord. You people are all an example of my work in the Lord.

1 CORINTHIANS 9:1 NCV

[Paul wrote:] We had the right to ask you to help us, but we worked to take care of ourselves so we would be an example for you to follow.

2 THESSALONIANS 3:9 NCV

Nothing is so contagious as an example. We never do great good or evil without bringing about more of the same on the part of others.

—FRANÇOIS DE LA ROCHEFOUCAULD

A man who lives right, and is right, has more power in his silence than another has by his words.

—PHILLIPS BROOKS

Anger

Tempering Your Temperament

Be angry, and do not sin. Meditate within your heart on your bed, and be still. —PSALM 4:4 NKJV

Mark could hardly believe what he was reading—an e-mail from the marketing department itemizing the materials that needed to be sent to a trade show halfway across the country next week. Not two months ago, a similar situation had occurred. The guys in the warehouse that Mark supervised had been expected to drop everything—all the other orders, all the demands from other departments—and pack up and ship two truckloads of materials in record time for an event the marketing department had known about for a year.

Furious, Mark was tempted to delete the e-mail. He wanted to claim he never got it. He wanted marketing to suffer. He wanted to teach them a lesson. He wanted to get even.

In his younger days, he would have. But his years of experience, and his new life in Christ, had taught him a thing or two about human nature: One, that responding in anger is never productive, and two, that an angry response is never well received. As a manager, he could now add number three—that a display of anger is not a good show to put on for the people on your team.

Instead, Mark said a quick prayer, counted to ten—well, twenty—and called his crew together to break the news. A few of the guys showed their temper and others groaned and complained, but once Mark settled them down, they turned their attention to the task at hand. They'd gotten through this before; they'd get through it again.

Mark's reaction to an infuriating request is commendable, but it didn't stop there. Once the work was done, the event was over, and marketing was basking in the glow of a successful show, Mark presented them with a proposal: Marketing would share their annual events calendar with him, and he would establish deadlines for placing orders and send reminders to a point person.

As Mark demonstrated, it's admirable when you can control your anger, but it's even better when you can use your anger as a springboard for action. Rightly used, a great deal of good can come from righteous, or justifiable, anger; anger over horrendous living conditions, for instance, has brought about much-needed change in inner-city slums and emerging-nations villages. The key is to keep your anger under control—control of the Holy Spirit, as Mark did when he stopped to pray.

If you think all anger is wrong, try to keep it in perspective. As long as your anger helps rather than hurts others, as long as you do not cross the line into sinful territory, as long as your anger serves as a reminder to turn to God—and as long as your anger does not negatively impact your team or your ability to lead them—then it's likely that you don't have a problem with anger after all—just with your perspective on it.

I Will

Control my emotions, with the help of the Holy Spirit.

yes _____ *no* _____

See justifiable anger as a springboard to action.

yes _____ *no* _____

Avoid the kind of anger that leads to sin.

yes _____ *no* _____

Turn to God as soon as anger arises in me.

yes _____ *no* _____

Find solutions to recurring problems that provoke me.

yes _____ *no* _____

Take a time out when I need to.

yes _____ *no* _____

Avoid negative displays of anger, especially around those I lead.

yes _____ *no* _____

Things to Do

☐ *Find a good resource on anger management, such as* The Anger Workbook *by Les Carter and Frank Minirth and use it.*

☐ *Use a Bible concordance to look up instances in which God became angry.*

☐ *Develop a routine for responding to anger (like Mark's: praying first, then counting to ten, and so forth).*

☐ *Think of a recent situation that made you angry and come up with three things you could do to prevent the same situation from occurring (or three ways you could better respond, if the situation is out of your control).*

☐ *Apologize to the recipients of any recent outburst of anger.*

☐ *Memorize any of the accompanying Scriptures on anger.*

Things to Remember

Be angry, and do not sin. Meditate within your heart on your bed, and be still.

PSALM 4:4 NKJV

A gentle answer will calm a person's anger, but an unkind answer will cause more anger.

PROVERBS 15:1 NCV

[Paul wrote:] My friends, do not try to punish others when they wrong you, but wait for God to punish them with his anger. It is written: "I will punish those who do wrong; I will repay them," says the Lord.

ROMANS 12:19 NCV

[Love] is not rude, it is not self-seeking, it is not easily angered, it keeps no record of wrongs.

1 CORINTHIANS 13:5 NIV

Stop being angry and don't try to take revenge. I am the LORD, and I command you to love others as much as you love yourself.

LEVITICUS 19:18 CEV

If you churn milk you get butter; if you pound on your nose, you get blood— and if you stay angry, you get in trouble.

PROVERBS 30:33 CEV

Temper is a weapon that we hold by the blade.

—SIR JAMES M. BARRIE

Speak when you are angry and you will make the best speech you will ever regret.

—AMBROSE BIERCE

Forgiveness

Mutual Gain

Bearing with one another, and forgiving one another, if anyone has a complaint against another; even as Christ forgave you, so you also must do.

—COLOSSIANS 3:13 NKJV

People of faith for the most part know that forgiving others is one of those things that the Bible is most clear about in its teachings: "Forgive, and you will be forgiven," Jesus said; "Forgive one another," Paul wrote. If someone hurts you in any way—physically, emotionally, even spiritually—God wants you to forgive that person, for your benefit as well as for the other person's benefit. If you lack forgiveness, you run the risk of harboring a bitter attitude, and you end up hurting yourself far more than the one who hurt you.

Every leader—including Jesus Himself—will be wronged by others at some point. It's the nature of the position you hold. Some people may resent you for the authority you have over them, no matter how good a leader you are, and may attempt to undermine that authority by stirring up dissension or spreading false reports about you or sabotaging your best efforts in any number of ways. You'll need to deal with those problems in a practical and decisive way, of course, but before you act, make sure you have forgiven the person in your heart.

Only then can you be certain that whatever action you take stems from a pure motive, one that places a high priority on mutual understanding and a restoration of the relationship. And if your adversary asks for your forgiveness, be sure to say those all-important words—"I forgive you"—out loud.

Forgiving your enemies comes much easier once you learn to live in an ongoing attitude of forgiveness. That means deciding ahead of time that no matter what another person does to you, you will extend forgiveness. Maybe you're in the middle of a long-term dispute right now, a conflict for which there is no end in sight. By cultivating a forgiving attitude—through prayer and the power of God's Spirit—you not only stand to resolve the dispute sooner but also will find it much easier to forgive your adversary should the conflict not be settled in your favor. That's what Stephen, the church's first martyr, did. Even as his enemies stoned him to death, he spoke from his own heart of forgiveness in asking God to forgive his executioners, echoing Jesus' words of forgiveness spoken from the cross.

You'll never regret extending forgiveness to another human being. The peace you gain will far outweigh the hurt your adversary caused, because in forgiving others you too are forgiven by God—and your relationship with Him will remain unbroken.

I Will

	yes	no
Forgive others, as I have been forgiven by God.		
Live in an ongoing attitude of forgiveness.		
Be a model for others of God's mercy and forgiveness.		
Decide in advance to forgive anyone who may hurt me in the future.		
Forgive my adversary before attempting to correct the problem.		
Work toward the restoration of any broken relationship.		
Recognize the harmful consequences of unforgiveness.		

Things to Do

☐ *List the names of those who may have wronged you recently and forgive them—out loud, to God.*

☐ *Read the story of the stoning of Stephen in Acts 7 and reflect on the way he modeled God's forgiveness to his executioners and to onlookers.*

☐ *Use a searchable on-line Bible to discover and read the many references to forgiveness just in the New Testament.*

☐ *For the next week, try cultivating an ongoing attitude of forgiveness in your everyday life, with your friends, family, and strangers, as well as those you lead.*

☐ *Select one of the accompanying verses on forgiveness from the Gospels and commit it to memory.*

Things to Remember

[Jesus said:] "In prayer there is a connection between what God does and what you do. You can't get forgiveness from God, for instance, without also forgiving others."

MATTHEW 6:14 THE MESSAGE

[Paul wrote:] Be gentle with one another, sensitive. Forgive one another as quickly and thoroughly as God in Christ forgave you.

EPHESIANS 4:32 THE MESSAGE

[Jesus said:] "Do not judge, and you will not be judged. Do not condemn, and you will not be condemned. Forgive, and you will be forgiven."

LUKE 6:37 NIV

[Luke wrote:] While council members were executing Stephen, he called out, "Lord Jesus, welcome my spirit." Then he knelt down and shouted, "Lord, don't hold this sin against them." After he had said this, he died.

ACTS 7:59–60 GOD'S WORD

Then Jesus said, "Father, forgive them, for they do not know what they do." And they divided His garments and cast lots.

LUKE 23:34 NKJV

It is in pardoning that we are pardoned.

—SAINT FRANCIS OF ASSISI

I can forgive, but I cannot forget, is only another way of saying, I will not forgive. Forgiveness ought to be like a canceled note— torn in two, and burned up, so that it never can be shown against one.

—HENRY WARD BEECHER

Ethics

Your Moral Compass

*He who walks with integrity walks securely, but he who
perverts his ways will become known.*

—Proverbs 10:9 NKJV

As a department manager with the state transportation
department, Harry wanted out of the bureaucratic
environment that seemed to stifle his every creative thought.
On a whim, he decided to sign up for an upcoming seminar
led by one of the many success gurus whose events had
proliferated across the country in recent years. Harry was
looking for a better life, and a better way to make a living, and
this man promised it.

Throughout the day-long event, Harry felt his spirits soar
higher and higher. One celebrity after another gave a stirring
talk about changing your life and being all that you could be
and overcoming every obstacle that stood between you and
your dream. By the end of the day, Harry was convinced—and
he bought $895 worth of the seminar leader's tapes and books
to prove it. From a distance, this man became Harry's mentor,
and Harry enthusiastically shared his teachings with anyone
who would listen, as well as many who preferred not to.

But then, the bottom fell out. Mr. Success was hauled off

to prison for fraud and securities violations. Harry was devastated. How could this happen? How could this man whom he admired turn out to be such a crook? Too late, Harry realized that in everything he heard and read, not one mention was made of the need for a code of ethics or a standard for moral leadership. As a believer, Harry had placed a high value on those qualities—and he was astonished to realize he had completely overlooked their absence in the life of his success mentor.

Harry had overlooked something else as well—the notion of guilt by association. Not criminal guilt, of course. But some of his colleagues wondered how Harry could have been so vulnerable to the teachings of a charlatan. His own staff seemed to have less regard for him.

Moral leadership involves both *being* an ethical leader and *following* an ethical leader. Harry's authority as an ethical leader was undermined by his allegiance to an unethical leader. Since every leader is also a follower, the character of the leader's leader is crucial to the influence, reputation, and authority to the follower; like it or not, people judge people by the company they keep.

Look at the person you consider your primary leader, perhaps a mentor or your boss or the head of an association. Even if you're at the top rung of your organization, you are a follower of *someone*. Has he proven himself to be honest and trustworthy and aboveboard in all his dealings, both personally and professionally? Is she someone whose character reflects the high standards you adhere to? In short, do they live according to sound moral principles?

That begs the question, what are sound moral principles? They're all over the Bible. If you have a red-letter Bible (one in which the words of Jesus are printed with red ink), read those portions and you'll have a solid foundation for moral living—and a standard by which to determine the character of your leader. If there's little evidence that the person you're following isn't at least trying to adhere to that standard, it's time to find a new leader. That won't change who the leader of your organization is, but it certainly should prompt you to shift your focus to a leader worth following.

Don't stop there—apply the same standard of moral character to yourself. Are you providing an example of ethical leadership for those who follow you? Use those red-letter sections to develop your own code of ethics, and communicate it to those under your authority. Explain that this is the standard you will be held accountable to, and you invite others to point out any blind spots you have with regard to your own standards. Then be prepared to graciously accept and act on those things that may be brought to your attention.

Above all else, make sure your role model is the ultimate example of moral leadership—Jesus Himself. Studying His life, His teachings, and His leadership style can't help but make you a better leader. Coupled with a life of prayer and a dependence on God, His example offers what you need to both *be* a leader and *find* a leader worth following.

I Will

Search out the Scriptures for guidance regarding
ethical behavior.

yes   *no*

Prove my trustworthiness by living according to a
high moral standard.

yes   *no*

Follow only those leaders whose character reflects
godly principles.

yes   *no*

Recognize Jesus as the ultimate example of moral
leadership.

yes   *no*

Trust God's Spirit to guide me in making ethical
decisions.

yes   *no*

Things to Do

☐ *Spend some time examining your ethics as they stand now. Ask God to
reveal any blind spots and seek His help in overcoming them.*

☐ *Start with the words of Jesus to develop your own written code of
ethics, followed by the Scripture reference (such as "I will not judge
others"—Matthew 7:1–2).*

☐ *Post your code, if appropriate, where others can see it, and ask them
to hold you accountable to it.*

☐ *Memorize—or meditate on—Psalm 1.*

☐ *Prepare a brief teaching on biblical ethics. (You may never give it
publicly, but preparing a lesson is one of the best ways to learn.)*

☐ *List those people you consider your leaders or role models. Compare
their ethics against those red-letter words of Jesus—and your own code
of ethics.*

Things to Remember

[Paul wrote:] You are witnesses, and God also, how devoutly and justly and blamelessly we behaved ourselves among you who believe.

1 Thessalonians 2:10 NKJV

The integrity of good people creates a safe place for living.

Proverbs 14:32 the message

> **The righteous man walks in his integrity; his children are blessed after him.**
> Proverbs 20:7 NKJV

Lord, who may abide in Your tabernacle? Who may dwell in Your holy hill? He who walks uprightly, and works righteousness, and speaks the truth in his heart.

Psalm 15:1–2 NKJV

[David wrote:] As for me, You uphold me in my integrity, and set me before Your face forever.

Psalm 41:12 NKJV

If we forgot the name of our God or stretched out our hands to pray to another god, wouldn't God find out, since he knows the secrets in our hearts?

Psalm 44:20–21 GOD'S WORD

[David wrote:] Create in me a clean heart, O God, and renew a steadfast spirit within me.

Psalm 51:10 NKJV

O LORD, You have searched me and known me. You know my sitting down and my rising up; you understand my thought afar off.

PSALM 139:1–2 NKJV

When Gentiles, who do not have the law, by nature do the things in the law, these, although not having the law, are a law to themselves, who show the work of the law written in their hearts, their conscience also bearing witness, and between themselves their thoughts accusing or else excusing them.

ROMANS 2:14–15 NKJV

A good man's mind is filled with honest thoughts; an evil man's mind is crammed with lies.

PROVERBS 12:5 TLB

[Paul wrote:] Now this is our boast: Our conscience testifies that we have conducted ourselves in the world, and especially in our relations with you, in the holiness and sincerity that are from God. We have done so not according to worldly wisdom but according to God's grace.

2 CORINTHIANS 1:12 NIV

[Paul said:] "Believe me, I do my level best to keep a clear conscience before God and my neighbors in everything I do."

ACTS 24:16 THE MESSAGE

It horrifies me that ethics is only an optional extra at Harvard Business School.

—SIR JOHN HARVEY

Let us raise a standard to which the wise and honest can repair; the rest is in the hands of God.

—GEORGE WASHINGTON

Networking

Better Than One

As iron sharpens iron, so a man sharpens the countenance of his friend.

—PROVERBS 27:17 NKJV

Networking—the buzzword of the 1990s turned lifestyle of the new millennium. The interaction among people both inside and outside an organization can have a profound and significant influence on its effectiveness in fulfilling its mission. But networking is a two-edged sword, and as a leader you have a responsibility to recognize both sides and make sure you and your team are aware of both the benefits and the pitfalls.

Side one. Networking can save time, provide valuable opportunities, and cut through the red tape that often hinders the progress of an organization's work. The more you and your team interact with each other and with people on the outside whose mission and focus is at the very least compatible with yours, the more likely you are to quickly generate much-needed ideas, find vital resources, inspire creative thought and action, and solve knotty problems. Likewise, you can help others in similar ways.

Side two. Networking can cut people down by making

them feel devalued. You've likely attended an event where you've observed "professional networkers" work the room with only one goal in mind: Getting whatever will serve their immediate purpose. These are the people who keep their eyes peeled for the movers and shakers—and who will drop their conversation with you in a heartbeat should a more "valuable" person walk by. The victims of their me-centered contact feel as if they've just been used. The truth is, they have.

In the 2003 book *Clout: Tapping Spiritual Wisdom to Become a Person of Influence*, written with his business partner Thomas G. Addington, author Stephen R. Graves provides insight into the Greek word *oikos*, which is often translated "house" but more accurately means "network"—a person's sphere of influence. Acts 20:20 speaks of Paul sharing Christ from "house to house." But what he was actually doing was networking, sharing the gospel by entering into a potential convert's sphere of influence—his world—and building relationships.

That's a pretty good model for you to follow as a leader. Encourage your people to build relationships, not just get what they can from a networking relationship and then move on. Do the same yourself, both within your organization and outside it. Show the people you meet how valuable they are as *people* and not just as contacts that can help your team do its work. By showing genuine concern for and interest in the people you and your team encounter, you'll be building a network of relationships that will outlast your immediate needs.

I Will

Draw on the wisdom and skills God has given other people.

yes _____ _no_ _____

Recognize the two sides to networking.

yes _____ _no_ _____

Acknowledge the value of each individual, regardless of their value as a networking contact.

yes _____ _no_ _____

Treat people with respect by giving them my full attention.

yes _____ _no_ _____

Seek to build relationships, not just a list of contacts.

yes _____ _no_ _____

Model respectful networking for my team.

yes _____ _no_ _____

Give freely to others as I network with them.

yes _____ _no_ _____

Things to Do

☐ *Make a list of do's and don'ts—or better, principles—your people need to keep in mind when networking.*

☐ *Read Clout, which expands on the idea of networking to include a person's many spheres of influence.*

☐ *Come up with ideas for two or three informal social events where the people in your organization can interact with each other (for large organizations) or with other groups (for smaller teams).*

☐ *Recall a time when you may have used that second side of the networking sword on someone else. Apologize and ask for forgiveness if possible; in any event, pray and ask God for forgiveness.*

☐ *Now recall a time when you were a victim of a networking sword. Forgive the one who wielded the sword, even if you can't remember the person's name.*

Things to Remember

[Paul wrote:] You yourselves are our letter, written on our hearts, known and read by everybody. You show that you are a letter from Christ, the result of our ministry, written not with ink but with the Spirit of the living God, not on tablets of stone but on tablets of human hearts.

2 CORINTHIANS 3:2–3 NIV

Dear friends, let us love one another, for love comes from God. Everyone who loves has been born of God and knows God.

1 JOHN 4:7 NIV

Love must be completely sincere. Hate what is evil, hold on to what is good.

ROMANS 12:9 GNT

Now you can have sincere love for each other as brothers and sisters because you were cleansed from your sins when you accepted the truth of the Good News. So see to it that you really do love each other intensely with all your hearts.

1 PETER 1:22 NLT

No man hath seen God at any time. If we love one another, God dwelleth in us, and his love is perfected in us.

1 JOHN 4:12 KJV

Respect for people is the cornerstone of communication and networking.

—SUSAN ROANE

To pursue success effectively, you must build supportive relationships that will help you work toward your goals. To build those relationships, you need to trust others; and to earn their trust, you in turn must learn to be trustworthy.

—STEDMAN GRAHAM

Health

Rx for Body, Soul, and Spirit

The LORD will strengthen him on his bed of illness; You will sustain him on his sickbed.

PSALM 41:3 NKJV

I'll sleep when I get to heaven. Maybe you've heard someone say those words. Maybe you've said them yourself. Either way, you know what it means: With so much to do here on earth, who has time to sleep? There's a world in need, a world that doesn't know God. Add to that the fullness of daily living—family, work, friends—and life comes close to a 24/7 activity, with sleep taking on a low priority. And that's bad news for your physical well-being, because without enough rest, anything else you do to stay healthy is significantly diminished.

You know the "healthy lifestyle" drill: Eat lots of fresh fruits and vegetables, watch your cholesterol level, avoid sugary junk foods, exercise at least three times a week, drink plenty of water, choose complex carbohydrates, and follow a host of specific suggestions depending on whose list you're looking at. Somewhere on every list is an item referring to the need for the right amount of sleep, but if you're like most Americans, your eyes tend to gloss right over that item. For a change, try putting the need for sleep at the top of the list.

The Bible calls your body the temple of God's Spirit (1 Corinthians 6:19). That's not just a figure of speech. Until the temple was destroyed in the first century, it was the sacred center of Jewish religious life. The laws for its maintenance and care were excruciatingly detailed. Any Jewish person—in fact, any person familiar with Jewish culture at the time—would have taken Paul's words very seriously. From a two-thousand-year distance, it's easy to give them less importance than some of Scripture's more "spiritual" instructions. Likewise the commandment to keep the Sabbath; that tends to fall on deaf ears in the twenty-first century.

Granted, religious people over the years have added one restriction after another to God's words about caring for the body. But that doesn't change the fact that God gave those words to benefit His people. He wants His people to be in optimal condition to do the work He has called them to do, and that means His people are also called to—that's right, *called* to—eat right, exercise, and get enough sleep. As a bonus, God gives His people a full day off every seventh day. Besides, there's a fairly decent chance there will be no need for sleep in heaven, which means you'd be wise to get your sleep right here on earth—the place where God provided an opportunity for physical rest.

I Will

	yes	no
Take care of the body God has given me.	_____	_____
Pay attention to my need for mental breaks.	_____	_____
Make time for spiritual renewal.	_____	_____
Appreciate a weekly day of rest as a gift from God.	_____	_____
Resist the temptation to work too long and too hard.	_____	_____
Recognize adequate rest as a non-optional element of life.	_____	_____
Be an example of healthy living for others.	_____	_____

Things to Do

☐ *Log your sleep pattern for at least a week and determine the ideal amount of sleep you should have to feel your best.*

☐ *Make a list of easy-to-prepare fresh fruits and vegetables that you like and place it on or near the refrigerator as a reminder when you make your grocery list.*

☐ *Take a physician-monitored treadmill stress test, or an on-line test on a medically reliable site (www.aafp.org, for example), to determine whether you are at risk for any number of stress-related disorders.*

☐ *Decide on an activity you enjoy that will get you moving—walking, running, biking, for example—and schedule a time to get started on it.*

☐ *Take a Sabbath rest—not the kind based on rules, but a simple day of rest to recharge your physical, spiritual, and emotional batteries.*

Things to Remember

Don't be impressed with your own wisdom. Instead, fear the LORD and turn your back on evil. Then you will gain renewed health and vitality.

PROVERBS 3:7–8 NLT

Do you not know that your body is a temple of the Holy Spirit, who is in you, whom you have received from God? You are not your own; you were bought at a price. Therefore honor God with your body.

1 CORINTHIANS 6:19–20 NIV

[John wrote:] Beloved, I pray that in all respects you may prosper and be in good health, just as your soul prospers.

3 JOHN 1:2 NASB

It is vain for you to rise up early, to sit up late, to eat the bread of sorrows; for so He gives His beloved sleep.

PSALM 127:2 NKJV

[God said:] "And you shall proclaim on the same day that it is a holy convocation to you. You shall do no customary work on it. It shall be a statute forever in all your dwellings throughout your generations."

LEVITICUS 23:21 NKJV

To insure good health: Eat lightly, breathe deeply, live moderately, cultivate cheerfulness, and maintain an interest in life.

—WILLIAM LONDEN

I don't eat junk foods and I don't think junk thoughts.

—PEACE PILGRIM

Teamwork

Making the Dream Work

Though one may be overpowered by another, two can withstand him. And a threefold cord is not quickly broken.

—Ecclesiastes 4:12 NKJV

When Margaret accepted a position as national director for a nonprofit organization dedicated to helping senior citizens acquire affordable health care, she considered it her top priority to resurrect a nationwide study of supplemental Medicare alternatives. The study had been foundering, she was told, because the team working on it had suffered steady attrition; the former director had found it difficult to recruit new members, and the current members were losing their focus and their interest.

After Margaret spoke privately with each person working on the study, she scheduled a group meeting. What she learned during their hour together confirmed what she had suspected during the individual interviews: This group was not a true team and never had been one. They were talented individuals working on the same project, but the concept of teamwork was not a reality in the work they were doing.

A veteran of the corporate world, Margaret had witnessed many failed attempts at teambuilding. She knew her strategy had to start from a foundation of trust—the one crucial element missing from all those unsuccessful efforts. So Margaret did just about the last thing anyone would have expected her to do, given the urgency of the situation: She arranged for the group to spend an afternoon at a nearby corporate retreat center, where they could relax and socialize and get to know one another as people. She followed that with another radical approach, assigning each person to spend a day or two outside the office talking to the seniors themselves. She instructed them not to return with statistics but with stories—stories they would tell each other.

Many of the stories the seniors told were heartbreaking. As they shared the stories with each other, the team became united in a common goal, one that now had names and faces attached to it. They returned to their work on the study with renewed vigor. As time passed, they began sharing their own stories with each other, stories about their elderly parents or grandparents who were facing the very problems their work was designed to correct. Margaret's strategy had succeeded; once they began to care about each other and trust each other, the group became a genuine team.

John C. Maxwell, who has written extensively on leadership and teambuilding, considers caring for one another the foundation upon which all other elements of teamwork are built. Those other elements—sharing a common goal, communicating with each other, and maintaining a spirit of cooperation—are important, but without genuine concern for each other, Maxwell believes, individuals are unlikely to make the sacrifices they may be called on to make in order for the team to be effective.

One quality you won't find on Maxwell's list—or Margaret's, for that matter—is conformity. Building a team requires a common vision, not a conforming mind-set. Successful leaders recognize creative thinking as a valuable contribution to any effort, and creativity can't thrive in an environment of conformity. Allowing team members to express themselves in their own unique ways not only greatly increases the possibilities for progress toward the ultimate goal but also underscores the trust you have in each member individually.

Look at the team Jesus assembled. They started out as a motley, even competitive, group of individuals in the Gospels, but they became a unified team that cared for each other and looked out for each other as the early church began to grow. Even a superficial reading of the Epistles reveals writers who had a unified message that they expressed in diverse ways. God trusted them to carry on Jesus' work and allowed them the freedom to be themselves as they worked toward the common goal of spreading the good news about Christ.

Margaret's approach may not work for you; a radical redirection may not be what your team needs right now. Ask God to show you that distinctive, unique, and creative approach you can take to turn your followers into the dream team every leader wants and needs to have. Pray for unity among your followers, that they may come to care for each other and work cooperatively rather than competitively. Most of all, show your team that you trust them—and that they, in turn, can trust you as their leader.

I Will

Pray for unity among those on my team.   *yes*   *no*

Promote cooperation by modeling it for those I lead.   *yes*   *no*

Understand that unity is not the same thing as
uniformity.   *yes*   *no*

Recognize the strengths of each member of my team.   *yes*   *no*

Get to know those I lead better than I do now.   *yes*   *no*

Build strong relationships among my followers.   *yes*   *no*

Encourage each person to contribute to the common
effort of the group.   *yes*   *no*

Things to Do

☐ *Read 1 Corinthians 12:12–26 and apply its truths about individual gifts and unity to your group.*

☐ *Begin defining the strengths of each member of your team, delegating the task to others as needed, if your group is large.*

☐ *Start praying one at a time for each of your followers, specifically that God would allow their gifts to flourish.*

☐ *Read John C. Maxwell's* The 17 Indisputable Laws of Teamwork: Embrace Them and Empower Your Team.

☐ *List some practical measures you can take to promote a cooperative spirit on your team, and implement at least one of them.*

☐ *Read the book of Nehemiah to learn how Nehemiah kept his team working in an effort to rebuild the temple.*

Things to Remember

Speaking the truth in love, [you] may grow up in all things into Him who is the head—Christ.

EPHESIANS 4:15 NKJV

Only let your conduct be worthy of the gospel of Christ, so that whether I come and see you or am absent, I may hear of your affairs, that you stand fast in one spirit, with one mind striving together for the faith of the gospel.

PHILIPPIANS 1:27 NKJV

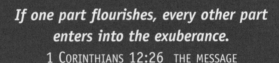

If one part flourishes, every other part enters into the exuberance.
1 CORINTHIANS 12:26 THE MESSAGE

The multitude of those who believed were of one heart and one soul; neither did anyone say that any of the things he possessed was his own, but they had all things in common.

ACTS 4:32 NKJV

He who serves Christ in these things is acceptable to God and approved by men. Therefore let us pursue the things which make for peace and the things by which one may edify another.

ROMANS 14:18–19 NKJV

[Shecaniah said to Ezra:] "Take courage, for it is your duty to tell us how to proceed in setting things straight, and we will cooperate fully."

EZRA 10:4 NLT

Two are better than one, because they have a good reward for their labor.

ECCLESIASTES 4:9 NKJV

Be of good comfort, be of one mind, live in peace; and the God of love and peace will be with you.

2 CORINTHIANS 13:11 NKJV

Have regard for good things in the sight of all men. If it is possible, as much as depends on you, live peaceably with all men.

ROMANS 12:17–18 NKJV

Behold, how good and how pleasant it is for brethren to dwell together in unity!

PSALM 133:1 NKJV

Don't repay evil for evil. Don't snap back at those who say unkind things about you. Instead, pray for God's help for them, for we are to be kind to others, and God will bless us for it.

1 PETER 3:9 TLB

There is one body and one Spirit, just as you were called in one hope of your calling.

EPHESIANS 4:4 NKJV

Coming together is a beginning, staying together is progress, and working together is success.

—HENRY FORD

Individual commitment to a group effort—that is what makes a team work, a company work, a society work, a civilization work.

—VINCE LOMBARDI

Humor

Serious Business

A merry heart does good, like medicine, but a broken spirit dries the bones.

—PROVERBS 17:22 NKJV

The concept was virtually unheard of: an airline whose corporate culture could best be characterized as focused on having fun. Airlines had traditionally been a bastion of professionalism—friendly, but still, highly professional. Then Southwest Airlines broke the mold, promising its employees that their hard work would be rewarded with a whole lot of fun on the job. Their antics have become the stuff of legend— throwing snacks at passengers, who played right along; making funny in-flight announcements; wearing not just casual but downright wacky costumes; even hiding in overhead compartments. Several other low-cost airlines have followed suit, including Delta's Song carrier, where the crew is referred to as the "talent."

That may not be your style, but your organization could be among those that do need to lighten up a bit. After all, Southwest is known for its employees' high productivity, estimated at 40 percent higher than at other airlines, and loyalty, which was tested in a tangible way during a series of layoffs. The fun their people had on the job made all the difference. And the fun even spilled over to the passengers.

You can introduce humor to your organization without going quite that far. Start by learning to laugh at your own foibles. Self-deprecating humor endears leaders to their team; by not taking themselves so seriously, they set a great example for their team to follow. Make light of those annoyances that normally tend to get on your nerves. It's not worth it to "sweat the small stuff," and the more you can see the humor in those situations, the more serious attention you can give to the big stuff.

Your sense of humor also allows your team to see your human side. All too often, leaders feel they must present a serious, all-work, no-play image. But play is as much a part of life as work is, and an important part at that. Many recent portrayals of Jesus have emphasized the lighter side of His nature. Some of the most serious Bible scholars have even begun to recognize the humor in some of the imagery He used, humor that would not have been lost on a first-century Jewish audience. A camel passing through the eye of a needle? We're so familiar with that and other images that we've forgotten what they must have sounded like the first time around.

There's one added benefit to a healthy sense of humor: the positive effect of laughter on your physical well-being. You no doubt want a productive, loyal, and healthy team. Try lightening things up a bit. And if you see your people tossing snacks at each other, you may want to join the team and play along.

I Will

Recognize humor as a way of dealing with truth. *yes* *no*

Realize that a healthy sense of humor can help keep *me* healthy. *yes* *no*

See the humor in daily situations that would ordinarily frustrate me. *yes* *no*

Use humor appropriately with those I lead. *yes* *no*

Encourage those in my organization to take minor problems lightly. *yes* *no*

Take a genuine delight in life. *yes* *no*

Things to Do

☐ *Go through the next few days consciously laughing at minor irritations, and notice how it changes your overall attitude.*

☐ *Pick up a compilation of humorous stories, such as* Nelson's Big Book of Laughter: Thousands of Smiles from A to Z, *to use when giving presentations.*

☐ *Visit a Web site dedicated to "holy humor," such as www.joyfulnoiseletter.com.*

☐ *Ask a trusted friend or colleague to identify one of your character traits that you need to take less seriously.*

☐ *Start a list of movies that make you laugh as a reminder to watch one when you need a shot of humor in your life.*

☐ *Learn how having a sense of humor can help you overcome illness and keep you healthy.*

Things to Remember

[Jesus said:] "Blessed are you who hunger now, for you shall be filled. Blessed are you who weep now, for you shall laugh."

LUKE 6:21 NKJV

He will yet fill your mouth with laughing, and your lips with rejoicing.

JOB 8:21 NKJV

Sarah said, "God has made me laugh, and all who hear will laugh with me."

GENESIS 21:6 NKJV

[God said:] "Then out of them shall proceed thanksgiving and the voice of those who make merry; I will multiply them, and they shall not diminish; I will also glorify them, and they shall not be small."

JEREMIAH 30:19 NKJV

A time to weep, and a time to laugh; a time to mourn, and a time to dance.

ECCLESIASTES 3:4 NKJV

He who is of a merry heart has a continual feast.

PROVERBS 15:15 NKJV

Those who went off with heavy hearts will come home laughing, with armloads of blessing.

PSALM 126:6 THE MESSAGE

Humor is something that thrives between man's aspirations and his limitations. There is more logic in humor than in anything else. Because, you see, humor is truth.

—VICTOR BORGE

People of humor are always in some degree people of genius.

—SAMUEL TAYLOR COLERIDGE

Positive Perspective

Winning Attitude

When you eat the labor of your hands, you shall be happy, and it shall be well with you.

—PSALM 128:2 NKJV

In his campaign for reelection, President Jimmy Carter frequently focused on America's problems, offering his proposed solutions. His opponent, Ronald Reagan, focused instead on the country's strengths, presenting his vision for bolstering its vitality. Though numerous other factors came into play, some political observers believe the nation's need at that time for an optimistic view of the future helped tip the scales in favor of Reagan, and voters elected him to be the one to lead the nation.

Optimism based on realistic expectations generates confidence and enthusiasm, exactly what you want to see in those you lead. Optimism based on wishful thinking—or worse, covering up the negative facts—will eventually backfire. That may result, at best, in disappointment among your followers or, at worst, in disastrous consequences for you and your organization. Your positive attitude needs to be anchored to realistic expectations shaped by your unwavering belief in your team's ability to overcome difficulties, coupled with your unshakable belief in God.

How can you be sure that your optimism is rooted in reality? It has become a clichéd image at this point, but it's still a valuable one in determining your viewpoint: the half glass of water. What people lose in the familiarity of the image is the *fact* that the eight-ounce glass contains four ounces of water. That fact does not change; only the pessimist's half-empty perspective against the optimist's half-full perspective is what changes. It's the way you look at and think about the facts that makes all the difference. The optimist—or, in your case, the optimistic believer—sees a half glass of water and anticipates the wonderful way in which God intends to fill it up to overflowing.

Look at the prevailing reality in your group or organization. Do you have a specific challenge that needs a fresh injection of optimism? Look at that challenge again in light of what God can do and your group's ability to overcome problems. Look forward to the wonderful way God intends to do far more than you can even imagine right now. Let that possibility sink deep into your spirit, and once it is settled there, convey your realistic optimism for the future to the rest of your team. Let them know that you're fully aware of the enormity of the challenge, but also let them know that you're fully confident in them and in the God you serve. Let that approach become your hallmark—and watch as your team tackles future challenges with confidence and enthusiasm.

I Will

Find the positive element in every situation and remain focused on it.

yes   _no_

Realize that my accomplishments depend in large part on my attitude.

yes   _no_

Believe that God is more powerful than any negative circumstance.

yes   _no_

Remember that it's just as easy to think positive thoughts as to think negative thoughts.

yes   _no_

Refuse to dwell on past failures and decide instead to anticipate future success.

yes   _no_

Foster a positive approach toward solving problems among members of my organization.

yes   _no_

Things to Do

☐ _Choose a particularly troubling situation in your life or work, and develop three or more action steps toward dealing with it._

☐ _Create a concrete mental picture of your overriding goal for the future so you can use it to replace negative images as they arise._

☐ _Begin training those in your organization to think in terms of positive solutions rather than negative problems._

☐ _Analyze a recent difficulty and write down the positive results, such as the lessons you learned from it._

☐ _Come up with creative responses to turn a team member's negative comments in a positive direction._

☐ _Create a list of "winning" habits that you need to work on, such as helping others, avoiding perfectionism, and spending time with God._

Things to Remember

[Paul wrote:] What happened to your positive attitude? It's a fact that if it had been possible, you would have torn out your eyes and given them to me.

GALATIANS 4:15 GOD'S WORD

You were taught to change the way you were living. The person you used to be will ruin you through desires that deceive you. However, you were taught to have a new attitude.

EPHESIANS 4:22–23 GOD'S WORD

The attitude you should have is the one that Christ Jesus had.

PHILIPPIANS 2:5 GNT

Good people enjoy the positive results of their words, but those who are treacherous crave violence.

PROVERBS 13:2 NLT

[Paul wrote:] We are hard pressed on every side, but not crushed; perplexed, but not in despair; persecuted, but not abandoned; struck down, but not destroyed.

2 CORINTHIANS 4:8–9 NIV

[Paul wrote:] If I am being poured out as a drink offering on the sacrifice and service of your faith, I am glad and rejoice with you all. For the same reason you also be glad and rejoice with me.

PHILIPPIANS 2:17–18 NKJV

If you have a positive attitude and constantly strive to give your best effort, eventually you will overcome your immediate problems and find you are ready for greater challenges.

—PAT RILEY

It takes but one positive thought when given a chance to survive and thrive to overpower an entire army of negative thoughts.

—ROBERT H. SCHULLER

Discernment

The Signs of the Times

Solid food belongs to those who are of full age, that is, those who by reason of use have their senses exercised to discern both good and evil.

—HEBREWS 5:14 NKJV

Diane's transfer to bank headquarters threatened to leave a noticeable void at the local branch where she worked. Her colleagues there had come to rely on her sound judgment. She had the remarkable ability to determine what actions would best serve both the bank's customers and its employees—at the same time. She skillfully walked a fine line between following established bank policies and making the best use of the flexibility and freedom branch managers were given. She could read the signs of the times—the omens that signaled change—and prepare her staff accordingly.

The quality her coworkers would miss most was the quality of discernment, which a good dictionary will tell you is a combination of insight and judgment. What the dictionary will not tell you is that discernment also has a spiritual dimension, which was especially operative in Diane's life. God had given her the ability to discern not just between right and wrong but also between right and right—or more accurately, between better and best. Diane was fully aware of the source of the gift, and she did her best to make sure she never misused it.

Beyond the dictionary definition, discernment involves a combination of many factors: common sense, sound thinking, the ability to learn from experience and apply those lessons to current situations, good decision-making skills, intuition, knowledge of Scripture, and deep reflection, all laid out before God through a lifestyle of continual prayer. That may sound like a lot for a leader to keep track of, but that's not how it works. Using your discernment may involve some conscious activity; mostly, though, it's a quality that is inherent in you, one of the qualities that set you apart for Christian leadership in the first place.

That doesn't mean, however, that it's a stagnant quality that needs no further development. Diane's case is a good example. She frequently asked God to make her more discerning, especially when it came to the sensitive issue of dealing with the employees she supervised. While she could immediately discern, for example, which employees needed closer attention, she found herself regularly going to God for answers to more specific questions: *I know Beth wasn't sick last Thursday—or even the last three times she called in sick. How do I handle this, God?* In that case, Diane learned "by chance" that Beth had a special-needs child but did not know how to ask for the time off that her child's care required. Diane was able to talk to her and assure her that the bank would work with her; Beth did not need to lie and feel guilty about it each time she called in sick.

As the branch employees continued to hope—and in some cases, pray—that her replacement would be just like Diane, they did not realize that Diane herself had become actively involved in choosing her successor. Working with the hiring manager at corporate headquarters, she culled through the applicants until she found just the right person. Her gift of discernment would continue on in the branch, in the person of the new manager, who embodied all the qualities she knew her staff had come to expect in her.

As a leader, you likely already have the gift of spiritual discernment. Whether or not you believe that to be true, you can ask God for the ability to be more discerning. As you read the Bible, be especially aware of the prominent role discernment plays in certain portions of Scripture, such as the book of Proverbs. Verses that offer a juxtaposition of good and bad—a wise person does *this*, but a foolish person does *that*—help sharpen your ability to discern. Likewise, many of the words Jesus spoke in the Gospels were intended to train His disciples to analyze the signs of the times, so that after He was crucified they would more clearly understand His mission and be better prepared to deal with the obstacles they would face as they tried to convince the world that He was, in fact, the long-awaited Messiah.

Use your gift of discernment wisely. With it, you can be confident in the decisions you are called on to make, knowing that God has placed within that single gift a combination of contributing factors and qualities that have gone into making you the leader you are.

I Will

Pray for the ability to discern between good and
evil, truth and untruth, and wisdom and foolishness. _yes_   _no_

Trust God to help me navigate my way through the
gray areas.   _yes_   _no_

Use the Bible as my standard for discerning right
from wrong.   _yes_   _no_

Help others distinguish between good and evil when
the choices are not clear cut.   _yes_   _no_

Ask God to give the gift of discernment to the
people in my organization.   _yes_   _no_

Things to Do

☐ Look up "discernment" in the dictionary and apply the definition to
your situation.

☐ Read the book of Colossians, in which Paul writes about wisdom and
discernment.

☐ List the tools available to you to discern God's will, such as prayer,
Scripture, God's Spirit, and so forth.

☐ Search for "discernment" on a Christian site like www.crosswalk.com
and read some of the resulting articles and devotionals.

☐ Analyze a recent problem in your organization and determine how it
could have been avoided had the parties involved been more
discerning.

Things to Remember

The word of God is living and powerful, and sharper than any two-edged sword, piercing even to the division of soul and spirit, and of joints and marrow, and is a discerner of the thoughts and intents of the heart.

HEBREWS 4:12 NKJV

[Paul wrote:] I pray that your love for each other will overflow more and more, and that you will keep on growing in your knowledge and understanding. For I want you to understand what really matters, so that you may live pure and blameless lives until Christ returns.

PHILIPPIANS 1:9–10 NLT

In all your ways acknowledge Him, and He shall direct your paths.
PROVERBS 3:6 NKJV

Some people don't have the Holy Spirit. They don't accept the things that come from the Spirit of God. Things like that are foolish to them. They can't understand them. In fact, such things can't be understood without the Spirit's help. Everyone who has the Spirit can judge all things. But no one can judge those who have the Spirit.

1 CORINTHIANS 2:14–15 NIrV

The LORD gives wisdom; from His mouth come knowledge and understanding.

PROVERBS 2:6 NKJV

Brothers and sisters, you are holy partners in a heavenly calling. So look carefully at Jesus, the apostle and chief priest about whom we make our declaration of faith.

HEBREWS 3:1 GOD'S WORD

[Paul wrote:] So we have continued praying for you ever since we first heard about you. We ask God to give you a complete understanding of what he wants to do in your lives, and we ask him to make you wise with spiritual wisdom.

COLOSSIANS 1:9 NLT

Be of the same mind toward one another. Do not set your mind on high things, but associate with the humble. Do not be wise in your own opinion.

ROMANS 12:16 NKJV

[David wrote:] True to your word, you let me catch my breath and send me in the right direction.

PSALM 23:3 THE MESSAGE

[Paul wrote:] I delight in the law of God after the inward man.

ROMANS 7:22 KJV

You may make your plans, but God directs your actions.

PROVERBS 16:9 GNT

Whoever can discern truth has received his commission from a higher source than the chiefest justice in the world who can discern only law.

—HENRY DAVID THOREAU

Discernment is God's call to intercession, never to faultfinding.

—CORRIE TEN BOOM

Commitment

The Power of Persistence

[Jesus said:] "But he who endures to the end shall be saved."

—MATTHEW 24:13 NKJV

Janet saw the handwriting on the wall and interpreted it accurately. As president of a small, local chapter of a national association of public speakers, she knew their charter was likely to be rescinded. Membership had fallen off, and their numbers had recently dipped below the minimum that was required to keep the chapter afloat. The members of the group genuinely liked each other and worked well together—and that, she reasoned, may have been part of the problem. They had become insular.

Resolved to keep the chapter alive, Janet began single-handedly recruiting new members—as well as volunteers from among the current membership who would mentor the new people. Furthermore, she began lining up paid speaking engagements for some of the more seasoned members of the chapter, something that fell clearly into the category of over and above the line of duty.

Though Janet worked largely in the background, the results of her efforts were evident, and a grateful membership responded enthusiastically to her commitment to keeping the chapter going. Soon, they began recruiting new members, and the mentoring program accomplished the desired effect of shifting the existing members' focus beyond their tight-knit group. The result? The chapter not only survived but also thrived and within two years became a model for growth and relationship-building for the entire association.

Janet's actions underscored four of the basic qualities of effective, committed leaders: They persevere through the rough times. They do what they want their followers to do. They know when to change course. They are personally invested in the work they do. But there's one more: They know when it's time to quit. That one didn't figure in to Janet's situation, because her team got on board with her. But if they hadn't, and if through prayer and reflection Janet had determined that the group no longer served the purpose for which it was intended, then she would have been in a position to make the difficult decision to let go. Propping up a team that has outlived its purpose is no better than giving up in defeat because you lack the commitment to keep it going.

The strength to persevere through the rough times ultimately comes from God, though your own personal resolve and the support of your team also factor in to the steadfastness of your commitment. Your team is looking to you as its leader to keep them pressing toward their goals even when the challenges seem insurmountable. Once you've determined that those goals are still valid, keep your eyes on them—and on God—and don't think about looking back.

I Will

Remain committed to my personal and
organizational mission.   _yes_   _no_

Surround myself with equally committed people.   _yes_   _no_

Realize that commitment from my team does not
mean conformity to a rigid set of ideas.   _yes_   _no_

Trust God to strengthen me when fatigue sets in.   _yes_   _no_

Remain joyful despite the obstacles.   _yes_   _no_

Know when to quit.   _yes_   _no_

Be open to Spirit-led changes in the program.   _yes_   _no_

Things to Do

☐ *Read about perseverance in James 1.*

☐ *Encourage someone who's having a rough time staying committed.*

☐ *Communicate your understanding of commitment to your team.*

☐ *Eliminate any activities that you are no longer committed to, if possible.*

☐ *Write out your mission statement to refer to when your sense of commitment begins to falter.*

☐ *Recommit yourself to your relationship with God, in prayer and on paper.*

☐ *Read an inspiring story of someone like cyclist Lance Armstrong who persevered against all odds.*

Things to Remember

[Paul wrote:] Since God has so generously let us in on what he is doing, we're not about to throw up our hands and walk off the job just because we run into occasional hard times.

2 CORINTHIANS 4:1 THE MESSAGE

[James wrote:] Consider it pure joy, my brothers, whenever you face trials of many kinds, because you know that the testing of your faith develops perseverance. Perseverance must finish its work so that you may be mature and complete, not lacking anything.

JAMES 1:2–4 NIV

> If you don't invest very much, then defeat doesn't hurt very much and winning is not very exciting.
>
> —DICK VERMEIL

[Nehemiah wrote:] So we built the wall, and the entire wall was joined together up to half its height, for the people had a mind to work.

NEHEMIAH 4:6 NKJV

We have become partakers of Christ if we hold the beginning of our confidence steadfast to the end.

HEBREWS 3:14 NKJV

> We would rather have one man or woman working with us than three merely working for us.
>
> —J. DABNEY DAY

May the God of all grace, who called us to His eternal glory by Christ Jesus, after you have suffered a while, perfect, establish, strengthen, and settle you.

1 PETER 5:10 NKJV

Prayer

Fuel That Keeps You Going

*Confess your trespasses to one another, and pray for one
another, that you may be healed. The effective, fervent
prayer of a righteous man avails much.*

—JAMES 5:16 NKJV

It's hard to imagine what your life as a leader would be
like if you did not have access through prayer to God and His
wisdom and guidance. The responsibility you feel toward the
people you serve is enough to keep you in constant
communication with God—never mind the myriad tasks you
must perform on a regular basis in order to continue serving in
your capacity as a leader. For a person who has no
understanding of the value of prayer, the road they travel must
be considerably more difficult to navigate.

The Bible, of course, has a great deal to say about prayer, as
do countless books on the subject, many of which provide
valuable insight into the role prayer plays in our relationship
with God. But at its basic level, there are really only two kinds
of prayer: a concentrated and focused conversation with God
that continues for a certain amount of time, and those quick,
urgent, middle-of-the-situation cries that you express to God in
the heat of the moment. Both kinds are valid, and either kind

can be spoken or thought. And Jesus modeled both kinds for His disciples.

The Lord's Prayer, found in Matthew 6:9–13, exemplifies a focused prayer. In offering that prayer as a model, Jesus was not only giving His disciples a set of specific words to speak, He was also showing them the need for a time of concentrated communication with God. In His cry from the cross—"Father, forgive them; for they do not know what they are doing" (Luke 23:34 NASB)—He issued an urgent cry straight from His heart— an example of the heat-of-the-moment prayer.

What's significant is that Jesus' urgent plea was rooted in those times of concentrated prayer—which at times lasted for hours or even all night. A heart of forgiveness, one that can ask God to forgive the executioners themselves, doesn't spring from a void. It springs from the times of focused prayer that create an unswerving trust and confidence in the God to whom those prayers are directed. Your heart is nurtured and strengthened and transformed in those times of thoughtful prayer, so that when a crisis hits, you can send out those spur-of-the-moment prayers with the utmost confidence that God hears them and that God will respond to them.

Always keep in mind that prayer is a two-way conversation with God—you need to give Him an opportunity to "speak" to you in response, by placing within you the wisdom to know how to pray and how to act on your prayer requests. And remember to approach prayer with an open mind. God's answers may not look at all like the answers you anticipate! Above all, pray—for wisdom, for your team, for every big and little thing in your life.

I Will

Set aside a regular, daily time for prayer.

_____ yes _____ no

Be vulnerable and honest with God.

_____ yes _____ no

Persevere in prayer even when I don't feel like it.

_____ yes _____ no

Pray individually for members of my team.

_____ yes _____ no

See prayer as a two-way conversation.

_____ yes _____ no

Learn to recognize unusual answers to prayer.

_____ yes _____ no

Pray in a variety of ways.

_____ yes _____ no

Things to Do

☐ Rewrite the Lord's Prayer (Matthew 6:9–13) in your own words.

☐ Start writing down Scripture verses that you can pray back to God.

☐ Set aside time on your calendar for a focused study of prayer.

☐ If permissible, set aside a regular prayer time for your team.

☐ Find a prayer partner and begin praying together.

☐ The next time you're forced to wait (such as in a doctor's office), write out a prayer to God about the situation.

☐ Start a notebook where you can begin to record answers to prayer.

Things to Remember

[God said:] "It shall come to pass that before they call, I will answer; and while they are still speaking, I will hear."

ISAIAH 65:24 NKJV

[Jesus said:] "If ye shall ask any thing in my name, I will do it."

JOHN 14:14 KJV

[Jesus said:] "Therefore I say to you, whatever things you ask when you pray, believe that you receive them, and you will have them."

MARK 11:24 NKJV

[Paul wrote:] Likewise the Spirit also helps in our weaknesses. For we do not know what we should pray for as we ought, but the Spirit Himself makes intercession for us with groanings which cannot be uttered. Now He who searches the hearts knows what the mind of the Spirit is, because He makes intercession for the saints according to the will of God.

ROMANS 8:26–27 NKJV

Be anxious for nothing, but in everything by prayer and supplication, with thanksgiving, let your requests be made known to God.

PHILIPPIANS 4:6 NKJV

In prayer it is better to have a heart without words than words without a heart.

—JOHN BUNYAN

Prayer is not a substitute for work, thinking, watching, suffering, or giving; prayer is a support for all other efforts.

—GEORGE BUTTRICK

Priorities

First Things First

[Jesus said:] "Seek first the kingdom of God and His righteousness, and all these things shall be added to you."
—MATTHEW 6:33 NKJV

Things were not going so well for Michael. He sat in the examining room, fidgeting with some forms he had to fill out, as he waited for the doctor to appear. He knew the news would not be good. His previous blood tests—three in the past year alone—had shown his cholesterol level to be dangerously high. Dr. Hamilton had put him on a strict low-fat diet and exercise regimen designed for weight loss and stress reduction, and advised him to cut back on his workload, at least until there was a noticeable improvement in his physical condition. Thinking back over the three months since his last visit, Michael figured he was in for a talking to.

He was right. His cholesterol level was well above 200, and he had not lost a single pound. As Dr. Hamilton grilled him, Michael admitted, point by miserable point, that no, he had not followed a single one of his instructions. That's when the tables turned on him: Michael was not just Dr. Hamilton's patient. He was also his pastor, and it was his turn to hear an impromptu sermon.

"What are your priorities? I want you to name them, one by one," his physician said. "Well, God, family, work, and then after that, I'm not sure," Michael said. "No. Those are not your priorities," Dr. Hamilton responded. "I've watched you for five years now, and I can tell you what your priorities are: Your work at the church takes the top three positions: putting out fires to avoid conflict with the members, making sure everyone else on the staff is doing their job, and, finally, getting your sermons and your other teachings together. Somewhere after all that comes your family and God, but I'm not even sure which order they're in. And your health isn't even on your list. Neither is rest or vacation time."

Michael resisted the urge to object. He knew his doctor—his friend, his parishioner—was right. Michael had given a theologically correct answer, but it did not line up with the reality of his daily life. What Dr. Hamilton said next surprised him. He "ordered" Michael to cancel all his appointments for the following day and get away from the church for the entire day. He was to spend the day alone with God, setting his priorities according to how God—and not Dr. Hamilton—directed him. The physician-ordered day off was a gift from the doctor; his rearranged priorities would be a gift from God.

Michael's theologically correct priority list probably mirrors yours. You know that God should come first in your life; after all, how many times have you counseled others to seek first the kingdom of God? And you know that your family should be your second priority. But it's a rare Christian leader who can honestly say that the work he or she does comes in at third place. Too often, church- or mission-related work takes first place, spills over into second place, and soon enough begins encroaching on third place. Family comes in a distant fourth or fifth—and that applies even if you're single. As long as you have living relatives, they are your family and need to be a priority in your life.

The tyranny of the urgent—or the seemingly urgent—rules the lives of far too many people. Don't be one of them. Understand that there are plenty of other people out there who are not only willing but also able to take up some of the slack when you realize you just can't do it all. Make sure your priorities are the important things in life, the things that matter most. Make sure your relationship with God is your top priority. Through that relationship—a genuine, intimate, wisdom-seeking relationship with God—your other priorities will fall into line. Like Michael, you may have to take off a day—or two or three—and spend some time alone with God, asking Him to help you prioritize your life, not just on paper but in reality. Living out those priorities will be a challenge, especially at first. But with God's help, the support of your family, and the understanding of those you lead, you'll find that living according to God's plan is far more satisfying—and productive—than living a life of skewed priorities.

I Will

Make sure God is my number one priority.   _yes_   _no_

Realize that one misplaced priority throws my life
off balance.   _yes_   _no_

Understand the difference between urgent and
important priorities.   _yes_   _no_

Be thankful for God's guidance in establishing
priorities.   _yes_   _no_

Avoid the temptation to do too much in any one
area of my life.   _yes_   _no_

Learn to make leisure one of my priorities.   _yes_   _no_

Things to Do

☐ *Prioritize the main areas of your life (God, family, church, work, and so forth) on paper.*

☐ *Analyze how well you've done in placing God Himself—not what you do for Him—in the top spot.*

☐ *Ask a close associate—or your spouse, if you dare!—if your priorities have been out of line lately.*

☐ *Train your team in prioritizing their life and work.*

☐ *Ask a colleague to keep you in check when you begin to require too much of those on your team.*

☐ *Ask forgiveness from anyone you've ignored who should be a priority in your life.*

☐ *Assess how you can better take care of your body, mind, and spirit.*

Things to Remember

Command those who are rich in the things of this life not to be proud, but to place their hope, not in such an uncertain thing as riches, but in God, who generously gives us everything for our enjoyment.

1 TIMOTHY 6:17 GNT

[Jesus said:] "Sell your possessions and give to the poor. Get for yourselves purses that will not wear out, the treasure in heaven that never runs out, where thieves can't steal and moths can't destroy. Your heart will be where your treasure is."

LUKE 12:33–34 NCV

> [Jesus said:] *"Stockpile treasure in heaven, where it's safe from moth and rust and burglars."*
> MATTHEW 6:20 THE MESSAGE

[Paul wrote:] You gain a lot when you live a godly life. But you must be happy with what you have. We didn't bring anything into the world. We can't take anything out of it. If we have food and clothing, we will be happy with that. People who want to get rich are tempted. They fall into a trap. They are tripped up by wanting many foolish and harmful things. Those who live like that are dragged down by what they do. They are destroyed and die.

1 TIMOTHY 6:6–9 NIrV

Trust in your wealth, and you will be a failure, but God's people will prosper like healthy plants.

PROVERBS 11:28 CEV

Come now, you who say, "Today or tomorrow we will go to such and such a city, and spend a year there and engage in business and make a profit." Yet you do not know what your life will be like tomorrow. You are just a vapor that appears for a little while and then vanishes away. Instead, you ought to say, "If the Lord wills, we will live and also do this or that."

JAMES 4:13–15 NASB

[Jesus said:] "You can't worship two gods at once. Loving one god, you'll end up hating the other. Adoration of one feeds contempt for the other. You can't worship God and Money both."

MATTHEW 6:24 THE MESSAGE

[Jesus said:] "Anyone who listens to my teaching and obeys me is wise, like a person who builds a house on solid rock. Though the rain comes in torrents and the floodwaters rise and the winds beat against that house, it won't collapse, because it is built on rock. But anyone who hears my teaching and ignores it is foolish, like a person who builds a house on sand. When the rains and floods come and the winds beat against that house, it will fall with a mighty crash."

MATTHEW 7:24-27 NLT

The older I get the more wisdom I find in the ancient rule of taking first things first, a process which often reduces the most complex human problem to a manageable proportion.

—DWIGHT D. EISENHOWER

We realize our dilemma goes deeper than shortage of time; it is basically a problem of priorities. We confess, "We have left undone those things that we ought to have done; and we have done those things which we ought not to have done."

—CHARLES E. HUMMEL

Change

Breaking with the Past

[The Lord said:] "Do not remember the former things, nor consider the things of old. Behold, I will do a new thing, now it shall spring forth; shall you not know it? I will even make a road in the wilderness and rivers in the desert."
—ISAIAH 43:18–19 NKJV

Breaking with the past was not something that came easily to Karen. After all, managing the mercantile store her grandparents founded in the mid-twentieth century smacked of tradition and the-way-we-always-did-it, if nothing else. For decades the shop had hummed along with a steady stream of customers in the quaint town she called home. But with a recent surge in tourist traffic eager to visit the restored downtown district, Karen knew it was time to take the family business to the next level.

She called a staff meeting to discuss changes they could make to the store—retaining its authentic flavor but reaching out to a new demographic. Before the meeting could turn into a noisy free-for-all of idea pitching, Karen led the staff in a prayer, asking God for guidance, creativity, and unity. She knew how important it was to foster team spirit among the staff and get everyone behind the same vision. The ideas that emerged from the meeting would require 100 percent effort on the part of the staff—and even more from Karen—but they agreed the extra work would be worth it if the plan for change was successful.

Change rarely comes easy. If you're like most leaders, you find a comfort zone where the organization or group you lead motors along, right on target for your projections. The only problem is that if you're not moving forward you're really moving backward—that middle ground of glorified inertia is essentially nonexistent.

Over two thousand years ago, another leader faced change he would have preferred not to deal with. Nehemiah found himself among a band of Jews who journeyed back to Jerusalem after their Babylonian captors set them free. The journey alone would have been enough to spark constant complaint, a long trek through a dusty desert region. But when the Israelites arrived at their beloved city, they discovered the walls in ruins. Rather than bemoan the state of the city, Nehemiah rose to the leadership challenge and organized a workforce to rebuild the broken walls. Like Karen, he looked to God for strength and inspiration, and he used his leadership gift to ignite a contagious enthusiasm for the work ahead.

Whether change is forced upon you or staring you in the face as a must-do, seize the reins of opportunity confident that God will inspire and equip you, as you in turn inspire and equip those who follow your lead.

I Will

Regard change as an opportunity for growth rather than a necessary evil.

yes   *no*

Realize that how I respond to change is my choice— and reflects my leadership personality.

yes   *no*

Find the positive in situations that are out of my control.

yes   *no*

Encourage those I lead through the transition phase of change.

yes   *no*

Ask God to make me pliable when change is either forced upon me or required of my leadership.

yes   *no*

Commit myself to approach change with an attitude of prayer first.

yes   *no*

Things to Do

☐ *Make a short list of major changes in your life that have turned out for good.*

☐ *To gain perspective, count how many times in one day you are affected by change outside your control.*

☐ *Write a what-if scenario of how a situation you're facing right now could turn out if you embrace change.*

☐ *Confide in a friend about your fears of change in a specific situation, and ask for their advice.*

☐ *Find someone you can mentor through successful change, based on your past experiences and leadership strengths.*

☐ *Write out a prayer of thanksgiving to God for His control of all things, and post it where you'll see it daily.*

Things to Remember

"Behold, the former things have come to pass, now I declare new things; before they spring forth I proclaim them to you."

ISAIAH 42:9 NASB

The jar he was making did not turn out as he had hoped, so the potter squashed the jar into a lump of clay and started again.

JEREMIAH 18:4 NLT

A new heart also will I give you, and a new spirit will I put within you: and I will take away the stony heart out of your flesh, and I will give you an heart of flesh.

EZEKIEL 36:26 KJV

A voice of one calling: "In the desert prepare the way for the LORD; make straight in the wilderness a highway for our God."

ISAIAH 40:3 NIV

Now is the time. Never forget the warning, "Today if you hear God's voice speaking to you, do not harden your hearts against him, as the people of Israel did when they rebelled against him in the desert."

HEBREWS 3:15 TLB

"I the LORD do not change."

MALACHI 3:6 NIV

Life is change.
Growth is optional.
Choose wisely.
—KAREN KAISER CLARK

I can't change the direction of the wind, but I can adjust my sails to always reach my destination.

—JIMMY DEAN

Security

On Solid Ground

You are of God, little children, and have overcome them, because He who is in you is greater than he who is in the world.

—1 JOHN 4:4 NKJV

The irony of leadership is that you must instill a sense of security in those you lead, even while you are floundering privately, calling out to God "What next?" It's been said that it's lonely at the top. Leadership never seems so lonely as those times when you feel you carry the burden of the entire organization on your shoulders while showing a brave face to the world.

You're in good company. When the apostle John penned those famous words in his first letter to the early church (1 John 4:4), he faced the opposition of Rome as a missionary for Christ. Yet his overwhelming sense of security in God superseded any physical constraints on his life. His words still resonate today with the confidence of one who knows he is in God's hands—what safer place could he be?

Intent on carrying the gospel into Western Europe, another apostle, Paul, boarded a ship for Rome, but a typhoon shipwrecked the vessel and Paul swam ashore—only to be bitten by a snake. He found himself stranded on the island of Malta for three months. Talk about an opportunity for frustration and insecurity! Yet his words in the Scriptures betray nothing but a man who has learned to entrust his life completely to God—including setbacks and crossroads. At the height of the storm, Paul told the terrified sailors: "I belong to God, and I worship him. Last night he sent an angel to tell me, 'Paul, don't be afraid! You will stand trial before the Emperor. And because of you, God will save the lives of everyone on the ship.' Cheer up! I am sure that God will do exactly what he promised" (Acts 27:23–25 CEV).

A life that is truly "hidden with Christ" (see Colossians 3:3 NKJV) is marked by peace and an abiding sense of security, no matter what befalls it. For the leader, that means even the times of uncertainty—times when you wish someone would show *you* the way—are in God's hands. True, God never promised you a life of uninterrupted ease, but His Word is replete with promises and images of security once you make Him your mainstay.

No matter what challenges your organization might be experiencing, no matter what disconcerting circumstances might be undermining the progress you need to make, know this: Whatever setbacks or situations face you today, God is in control. Remember that your life and times are secure in the hands of God. And if God is truly your foundation in life, you will always be on solid ground. No troubling state of affairs can possibly change that.

I Will

Remind myself daily that my security comes from the Lord.

yes _____ _no_ _____

Reflect on what it means to be "on solid ground" when everything around me seems out of control.

yes _____ _no_ _____

Trust God for the little things as well as the big things in my leadership role.

yes _____ _no_ _____

Be conscious of how a godly man or woman I respect handles times of insecurity.

yes _____ _no_ _____

Take comfort in God's promise of security for me.

yes _____ _no_ _____

Reflect on stressful matters so that I can give them over to God.

yes _____ _no_ _____

Things to Do

☐ _Read Acts 27–28 and note the number of setbacks Paul endured and his godly response to them._

☐ _Make a list of things keeping you from a peace-filled life, and turn them over to God one by one._

☐ _Think of a time when you felt overwhelmed in your leadership, but God came through with the right solution._

☐ _Ask God for an abiding sense of security in Him today._

☐ _Seek out a mentor who has modeled "solid ground" leadership in times of insecurity._

☐ _Take the words of Paul to heart, and reassure someone you lead that God is with them too._

Things to Remember

I have been young, and now am old; yet I have not seen the righteous forsaken, nor his descendants begging bread.

PSALM 37:25 NKJV

GOD, my shepherd! I don't need a thing.

PSALM 23:1 THE MESSAGE

Young lions may go hungry or even starve, but if you trust the Lord, you will never miss out on anything good.

PSALM 34:10 CEV

For the LORD your God is bringing you into a good land—a land with streams and pools of water, with springs flowing in the valleys and hills.

DEUTERONOMY 8:7 NIV

Here is something to remember. The one who plants only a little will gather only a little. And the one who plants a lot will gather a lot.

2 CORINTHIANS 9:6 NITV

"Therefore do not worry, saying, 'What shall we eat?' or 'What shall we drink?' or 'What shall we wear?' "

MATTHEW 6:31 NKJV

Happiness has many roots, but none more important than security.

—E. R. STETTINIUS

There is no security on this earth, there is only opportunity.

—GENERAL DOUGLAS MACARTHUR

Self-Discipline

Who's In Control Here?

To knowledge [add] self-control, to self-control perseverance,
to perseverance godliness.

—2 PETER 1:6 NKJV

A strong leader is a self-disciplined leader, regardless of the
mission or track record of the organization they lead. Can you
imagine leaders who demand discipline and line-toeing by
their team but eschew the rules themselves? Such leaders foster
little respect. Contrast that with a leader who practices self-
control day in and day out. Others may watch for them to trip
up, but the habit of self-discipline is so ingrained in them that
it's become second nature—or, perhaps, their new nature in
Christ.

The ability to govern oneself in a right manner is
foundational to success in leadership. Self-discipline in
leadership can run a large gamut, from avoiding situations that
hint at sexual impropriety, to arriving at work on time, to
keeping your business ethics accountable to a mentor. Anyone
who seeks to lead in a God-honoring way will discover, as the
apostle Peter did, that self-discipline begets perseverance,
which in turn begets godliness.

In the movie *Master and Commander*, actor Russell Crowe
depicts a sea captain who is both respected and well liked, but

Captain Jack Aubrey is not above disciplining a sailor who shows insubordination to a ranking officer. In a private conversation with the weak-kneed midshipman, he encourages the man to show strong leadership and to follow his own example. Captain Jack consistently puts the needs of his ship—and the larger mission of serving the British empire—before his own needs or preferences, exemplifying self-discipline in action. He knows that any team instinctively respects a leader who sets rules and then follows them himself. The men do indeed respect Captain Jack and even call him "Lucky Jack" for his reputation of bringing the *Surprise* through the worst of storms intact.

Larry felt the temptation to let his eyes wander every day at the office. One of the women in his department wore provocative clothing, despite the corporate dress code and at least two previous warnings. It didn't help that she was attractive. Being the boss, Larry knew he had to set a godly example among the men on his team. Whenever he addressed the woman, he looked her in the eye and treated her as a person, not an object. And though he heard the snickers from the other males, he refused to take part in their coarse jesting behind the woman's back.

Finally, Larry asked the personnel director—a woman—to intervene and give the female employee an ultimatum: either adhere to the company wardrobe of modest dress or be out of a job. When she realized he meant business, the woman changed her mode of dress, and the other men started treating her with more respect. Although he remained behind the scenes throughout the situation, Larry knew he'd taken the high road—and kept his own thoughts and actions clean.

The apostle Paul couldn't emphasize self-control often enough among the early churches he wrote to in his letters. To the Christians in Galatia he implored, "So I say, live by the Spirit, and you will not gratify the desires of the sinful nature. For the sinful nature desires what is contrary to the Spirit, and the Spirit what is contrary to the sinful nature. . . . The acts of the sinful nature are obvious: sexual immorality, impurity and debauchery; idolatry and witchcraft; hatred, discord, jealousy, fits of rage, selfish ambition, dissensions, factions and envy; drunkenness, orgies, and the like. I warn you, as I did before, that those who like this will not inherit the kingdom of God" (Galatians 5:16–17, 19–21 NIV).

What was fitting for a godly leader in the time of the apostles has not changed with the progression of time. Like the men and women of Paul's day, you live in a culture given to self-indulgence, one that denies few pleasures. But in the midst of this worldly indulgence you stand out like a beacon on a hill, showing a better way for those who want to live moral lives.

Stop and take inventory of your own leadership right now. Have you faced situations in which you could have bent the rules for yourself—and no one would have been the wiser? The temptation to exempt yourself from unpleasant tasks, for whatever reason, is a constant threat to leaders. But if you govern your life, your leadership, and your organization by the Golden Rule book, you will always earn the respect and admiration of those you lead.

I Will

Allow God to reveal areas of my life where I lack
self-control.   _yes_   _no_

Trust God to help me live a life of self-discipline
both in private and in front of those I lead.   _yes_   _no_

Realize that I will make mistakes, but not be afraid
to admit those mistakes.   _yes_   _no_

Determine to practice self-discipline in my
leadership role.   _yes_   _no_

Realize that others look to me as a role model and
take that responsibility seriously.   _yes_   _no_

Things to Do

☐ *Reflect on two or three times when you didn't practice self-discipline.
Recast those scenarios with a positive outcome—what you would do
differently if you could do them over again.*

☐ *Write out an action plan detailing two or three things you can do daily
to stay on the high road of self-discipline.*

☐ *Ask God for the strength to exercise self-discipline when temptations
arise.*

☐ *Confide in a mentor about the one area you struggle with most in your
leadership.*

☐ *Pinpoint any gray areas of self-control, and have your accountability
partner ask you about them weekly.*

☐ *Read the story of Joseph in the Old Testament to see how he handled
tempation as a leader (Genesis 39).*

Things to Remember

God is my strong fortress; he has made my way safe.

2 SAMUEL 22:33 NLT

No temptation has overtaken you except such as is common to man; but God is faithful, who will not allow you to be tempted beyond what you are able, but with the temptation will also make the way of escape, that you may be able to bear it.

1 CORINTHIANS 10:13 NKJV

> They want to be teachers of the law, but they do not know what they are talking about or what they so confidently affirm.
>
> 1 Timothy 1:7 NIV

I say then: Walk in the Spirit, and you shall not fulfill the lust of the flesh.

GALATIANS 5:16 NKJV

Now that Jesus has suffered and was tempted, he can help anyone else who is tempted.

HEBREWS 2:18 CEV

Now to Him who is able to keep you from stumbling, and to present you faultless before the presence of His glory with exceeding joy.

JUDE 24 NKJV

Blessed is a man who perseveres under trial; for once he has been approved, he will receive the crown of life which the Lord has promised to those who love Him.

JAMES 1:12 NASB

He gives strength to the weary, and to him who lacks might He increases power.

ISAIAH 40:29 NASB

The LORD will give strength to His people; the LORD will bless His people with peace.

PSALM 29:11 NKJV

I've banked your promises in the vault of my heart so I won't sin myself bankrupt.

PSALM 119:11 THE MESSAGE

Be careful! Watch out for attacks from the Devil, your great enemy. He prowls around like a roaring lion, looking for some victim to devour. Take a firm stand against him, and be strong in your faith. Remember that your Christian brothers and sisters all over the world are going through the same kind of suffering you are.

1 PETER 5:8–9 NLT

He that would govern others, first should be the master of himself.

—PHILIP MASSINGER

He who reins within himself and rules passions, desires, and fears is more than a king.

—JOHN MILTON

Self-Esteem

Blurred Vision

[The Lord said:] "Before I formed you in the womb I knew you; before you were born I sanctified you; I ordained you a prophet to the nations."

—Jeremiah 1:5 NKJV

Every day before she stepped out the door, Tracie stared at her reflection in the mirror and repeated five words. As she uttered them out loud, she remembered who she was, and the daily ritual fortified her for the hours ahead.

Being a dance instructor at a prestigious school might have bolstered most people's self-esteem, but Tracie battled a very public problem: her weight. Though a gifted teacher, she had gained unwanted pounds in the years following her performance career, and she worried that the other teachers—and her students—secretly derided her for it. She was no longer the lithe and slender size 8 that she had been for years. Now she had nearly doubled her dress size. Even though she could still execute a fine performance and give excellent instruction, she was embarrased and had to work to avoid feeling like a failure.

Self-esteem issues seem like the last thing that should be on the minds of leaders. After all, gifted leadership equals natural confidence, right? Not always. In fact, God seems to specialize in calling people of seeming inconsequence—the shy ones, the awkward ones, the misfit ones—to accomplish great things in His name. Take another look at Jeremiah, who tried to argue with God that he was too young to be a prophet, or Moses, who was slow of speech and begged God to let his brother Aaron be his mouthpiece.

When you look in the mirror, what do you see? Do you see a man or woman who has too many flaws to count, and do you dwell on them, bemoaning your deficiency? Or do you see yourself as the leader God has called at a specific time to a specific place for a specific purpose? Do you see what God sees?

A fellow dance instructor noticed the way Tracie glanced down whenever she passed other teachers in the hall, yet he had seen the fruit of Tracie's labors. Her excellent teaching had turned out some of the school's finest dancers. He had also heard of Tracie's compassionate one-on-one sessions with students who battled self-esteem issues of their own. Without realizing it, Tracie had become a wounded healer—and he told her so, encouraging her to let her inner light shine bright.

Like Tracie, when you begin to see God, and not yourself, reflected back in the mirror, you're becoming the best kind of leader of all, one who yields his or her talent to God's will and direction. Those five words Tracie repeated? "Not me, but the Lord."

I Will

Remember that I am made in the image of
Almighty God.   *yes*   *no*

Reflect on what it means for others to see Christ
in me.   *yes*   *no*

Allow God to open my eyes to the leadership gifts
and talents He has blessed me with.   *yes*   *no*

Determine to view myself as an instrument in the
Lord's hands, put here for a special purpose.   *yes*   *no*

Get reacquainted with the art of comforting others
with low self-esteem as God comforts me.   *yes*   *no*

Believe that God uses flawed individuals (like me)
to bring about His perfect will.   *yes*   *no*

Things to Do

☐ *Put a note on your bathroom mirror or computer monitor that says
"not me, but the Lord" or some similar self-esteem prompter.*

☐ *Write down five things you like about yourself and your leadership
ability.*

☐ *Ask God to give you confidence in your leadership role today.*

☐ *Read The Leader in You by Dale Carnegie, and note specific actions you
can take toward leading with confidence.*

☐ *Memorize 1 John 3:1 (NKJV): "Behold what manner of love the Father
has bestowed on us, that we should be called children of God."*

☐ *Confide in a friend the self-esteem issues you struggle with most, and
enlist them as your prayer partner.*

Things to Remember

God created man in His own image; in the image of God He created him; male and female He created them.

GENESIS 1:27 NKJV

Aren't two sparrows sold for only a penny? But your Father knows when any one of them falls to the ground. Even the hairs on your head are counted. So don't be afraid! You are worth much more than many sparrows.

MATTHEW 10:29–31 CEV

Now if we are children, then we are heirs—heirs of God and co-heirs with Christ, if indeed we share in his sufferings in order that we may also share in his glory.

ROMANS 8:17 NIV

I thank you, High God—you're breathtaking! Body and soul, I am marvelously made! I worship in adoration—what a creation!

PSALM 139:14 THE MESSAGE

This precious treasure—this light and power that now shine within us—is held in perishable containers, that is, in our weak bodies. So everyone can see that our glorious power is from God and is not our own.

2 CORINTHIANS 4:7 NLT

In my day, we didn't have self-esteem, we had self-respect.

—JANE HADDAM

Until you value yourself you will not value your time. Until you value your time, you will not do anything with it.

—M. SCOTT PECK

Simplicity

Paring Down

[Jesus said:] "Assuredly, I say to you, unless you are converted and become as little children, you will by no means enter the kingdom of heaven."

—MATTHEW 18:3 NKJV

For several years, Dennis got caught up in the glitz game with his coffeehouse, investing more than he could afford in cool décor and marketing frills to compete with a national chain. His colors were brash and beautiful; his chrome sleek and shining; his tables splashed with eye-catching designs. But now the overspending was catching up with him. As he looked over the last month's spreadsheet one more time, he rubbed his eyes and prayed a prayer of frustration: "God, I need your help . . . fast." If God didn't help him, what would he do? He was at his wit's end.

Then he did something radical for him—he actually listened for an answer. Over the next few hours, Dennis kept hearing one refrain in his mind: "Pare down. Get back to your original mission. People, not profits."

Pare down? He examined the ways he could do that and finally decided to offload some expensive equipment that was more aesthetic than functional. After all, he didn't need the flashiest and most impressive machines—he simply needed functional machines that could produce high-quality menu items. And he didn't need the cozy but costly marble-topped tables and ice-cream parlor chairs. Wood tables and padded chairs cost much less, and he found that they were even more comfortable for his customers. After Dennis scaled back his equipment, he set an advertising budget he could afford—he cut it by nearly two-thirds. Last, he opened his coffeehouse to the local Christian artists community and sponsored everything from poetry readings and art shows and book signings to spontaneous gatherings of several groups in his church.

Stripped of some of its trappings, the coffeehouse ironically appealed more to the art crowd than it had before. And now Dennis mingled among his customers—got to know them by name and greeted them as friends. He enjoyed the changes and felt that he had turned the corner in his business style.

Simplicity in leadership means different things to different people and will largely be defined by the nature of your organization. But following Dennis's lead might be a good place to start. Set aside an hour in your schedule this week to talk to God. Ask Him what areas you need to simplify, and really listen for His answers.

I Will

Choose to simplify rather than complicate my organization and its mission.

yes   *no*

Remember that simplicity is always more profound than complexity.

yes   *no*

Listen for God's input on how to get back to your original mission.

yes   *no*

Be aware of activities that bring refreshment and those that wear me down.

yes   *no*

Remember that money cannot buy happiness, peace, or guaranteed success in business.

yes   *no*

Keep my eyes on the big picture, and make a conscious choice to live in it.

yes   *no*

Things to Do

☐ *De-clutter your workplace and your mind today.*

☐ *Make a list of ways you can pare down financially in your organization.*

☐ *Now make a list of things you can do to get back to your original mission.*

☐ *Clear your schedule for one hour of concentrated "listening prayer" this week.*

☐ *Read a book on living simply, such as* The Simple Living Guide *by Janet Luhrs or* Complete Idiot's Guide to Simple Living *by Georgene Lockwood.*

☐ *Write a list of the things that demand your time, and ask God to show you which ones are important and which can go.*

Things to Remember

These things we write to you that your joy may be full.

1 JOHN 1:4 NKJV

They worshiped together at the Temple each day, met in homes for the Lord's Supper, and shared their meals with great joy and generosity.

ACTS 2:46 NLT

At that time Jesus, full of joy through the Holy Spirit, said, "I praise you, Father, Lord of heaven and earth, because you have hidden these things from the wise and learned, and revealed them to little children. Yes, Father, for this was your good pleasure."

LUKE 10:21 NIV

LORD, my heart is not haughty, nor my eyes lofty. Neither do I concern myself with great matters, nor with things too profound for me.

PSALM 131:1 NKJV

I'm asking the Lord for only one thing. Here is what I want. I want to live in the house of the Lord all the days of my life. I want to look at the beauty of the Lord. I want to worship him in his temple.

PSALM 27:4 NIrV

> To simplify complications is the first essential of success.
>
> —GEORGE EARLE BUCKLE

> When the solution is simple, God is answering.
>
> —ALBERT EINSTEIN

Vision

The Long View

Chasten your son while there is hope, and do not set your heart on his destruction.

—PROVERBS 19:18 NKJV

It's a bedrock truth of leadership: Before you can inspire others with a vision, you have to be inspired yourself—enough so that your vision catches fire and ignites enthusiasm in those you lead.

Nobody wants to be forced to work toward a goal they don't believe in. That's why successful leaders are best known for their ability to rally support for a vision, perhaps more than anything else. The wisest man who ever lived knew how important a shared vision is. He wrote, "Where there is no vision, the people perish" (Proverbs 29:18 KJV). God evidently put His stamp of approval on Solomon's words, for they became part of Scripture.

Think for a moment how powerful those words are: Without a vision, human beings *perish*—or wither away into a meaningless existence marked only by the dull hum of everyday routine. Can you imagine what your life would be like without a sense of destiny? How long could you sustain enthusiasm for a project—for life—if you were not inspired by a dream or big-picture view of what you wanted to accomplish? Most likely, without consciously thinking about it, you are fueled by your desire to achieve the dreams God set in your heart. That desire is a divine gift that you as a leader are equipped to share with others.

The book of Joshua in the Old Testament tells the story of another leader who was fired with a vision of what God wanted to accomplish through him and those he led. In the first chapter of Joshua, God gives the people of Israel a word picture of the Promsied Land they've waited so long to possess. Three times in the first nine verses the Lord says, "Be strong and courageous!" adding, "do not be discouraged, for the LORD your God will be with you wherever you go." Joshua's trust in the Lord and his inspired leadership gave the people a strong figure to follow, even as the threat of walking into enemy territiory sourrounded them on all sides.

Gail saw up close and personally how important it is to inspire a vision when she faced her first big goal as a Girl Scout troop leader: to raise $1,000 for a national charity through local fund-raisers. To twelve-year-old girls, $1,000 sounds like an impossible sum to raise—especially when your primary means of raising cash are car washes and bake sales.

When Gail told her troop about the goal of raising money, the girls listened but then just as quickly forgot as the distractions of boy-talk and that night's Girl Scout craft took over. Week after week Gail reminded the girls of the approaching deadline, but the girls didn't take ownership of the vision until something unexpected happened. That night at the meeting the girls noticed that one member was missing. Gail told them the girl's father was in the hospital, diagnosed with the same terminal illness they were raising funds for. She asked the troop to pray for his recovery and then asked how they wanted to raise funds for the charity.

Suddenly the goal of raising $1,000 consumed the troop. The girls rallied around the vision and threw themselves into their fund-raisers, surpassing the monetary goal and surprising themselves in the process.

Taking the long view in a project or organization means just what it sounds like: keeping your eyes on the horizon, or the big picture of what you set out to do. Even though the girls in Troop 1777 enjoyed fellowship and fun activities together, Gail helped to focus their attention on a worthy goal—with a real-life application—and taught them a lesson they would never forget. Something worth dreaming about is also worth working hard for.

God wisely put a yearning within you, and those you lead, to stretch toward something greater than yourself. When you add divine purpose to that sense of calling, the vision is still greater. As a leader, God has given you a divine mandate to be the vision caster, the one who rallies the team behind a dream, and then carries it through to fruition. Consider that calling a privilege!

I Will

Realize the importance of casting a vision for those
I lead.   _yes_   _no_

Allow God to prioritize my goals for the organization
I lead.   _yes_   _no_

Believe that God will reveal the vision most
important for me to pursue.   _yes_   _no_

Trust that God will help me vision-cast with
enthusiasm and a sense of purpose.   _yes_   _no_

Accept that occasionally my vision will get
sidetracked by things beyond my control.   _yes_   _no_

Things to Do

☐ *Ask God what His vision for your organization is. Write down His answer.*

☐ *Write out a clearly defined course of action for how you will realize that dream or vision.*

☐ *Set a timeframe for reaching the goal.*

☐ *Read Philippians 3 as if you're reading it for the first time. Note what Paul says about setting worthy goals.*

☐ *Ask a friend to pray for you to inspire a shared vision among those you lead.*

☐ *Have lunch with a trusted friend, and share your deepest thoughts about the vision you carry.*

Things to Remember

Where there is no vision, the people perish: but he that keepeth the law, happy is he.

PROVERBS 29:18 KJV

Then the LORD said to me, "Write my answer in large, clear letters on a tablet, so that a runner can read it and tell everyone else. But these things I plan won't happen right away. Slowly, steadily, surely, the time approaches when the vision will be fulfilled. If it seems slow, wait patiently, for it will surely take place. It will not be delayed."

HABAKKUK 2:2–3 NLT

> "Therefore . . . I was not disobedient to the heavenly vision."
>
> Acts 26:19 NKJV

Let us fix our eyes on Jesus, the author and perfecter of our faith, who for the joy set before him endured the cross, scorning its shame, and sat down at the right hand of the throne of God.

HEBREWS 12:2 NIV

The noble man makes noble plans, and by noble deeds he stands.

ISAIAH 32:8 NIV

We make it our aim, whether present or absent, to be well pleasing to Him.

2 CORINTHIANS 5:9 NKJV

My child, hold on to wisdom and good sense. Don't let them out of your sight. They will give you life and beauty like a necklace around your neck.

PROVERBS 3:21–22 NCV

Wisdom is in the presence of the one who has understanding, but the eyes of a fool are on the ends of the earth.

PROVERBS 17:24 NASB

We aren't making outrageous claims here. We're sticking to the limits of what God has set for us. But there can be no question that those limits reach to and include you.

2 CORINTHIANS 10:13 THE MESSAGE

As long, then, as that promise of resting in him pulls us on to God's goal for us, we need to be careful that we're not disqualified.

HEBREWS 4:1 THE MESSAGE

Christ has shown me that what I once thought was valuable is worthless. Nothing is as wonderful as knowing Christ Jesus my Lord. I have given up everything else and count it all as garbage. All I want is Christ.

PHILIPPIANS 3:7–8 CEV

The only limits are, as always, those of vision.

—JAMES BROUGHTEN

If you would hit the mark, you must aim a little above it; Every arrow that flies feels the attraction of earth.

—HENRY WADSWORTH LONGFELLOW

Wisdom

Your Greatest Asset

If any of you lacks wisdom, let him ask of God, who gives to all liberally and without reproach, and it will be given to him.
—JAMES 1:5 NKJV

A young man grows up in a wealthy household, pampered with everything his heart desires. No luxury is too great, for this is the son of a king. Yet, despite all the trappings of wealth and prestige, the young man is taught godly virtues from the time he can crawl. He learns the words of God at his mother's knee, and they sink deep roots into his heart where they will bear fruit one day.

Eventually the young man grows into maturity, and the day comes when he ascends to his father's throne. Unlike other kings, he remembers the teachings of his youth, and he talks with God often. Pleased with the new king's devout heart, God tells him He will give him whatever he desires. The king might ask God for endless monetary success or long life, but instead he asks for wisdom. He asks the Lord's help that he might rule the people with understanding.

Get wisdom? Those aren't words you hear too often these days, but anyone who aspires to godly leadership will seek this treasure. Every day you face choices and situations that test the mettle of your leadership. How you respond in the midst of leadership crises shows your true colors and can mean the difference between success or mediocrity.

Each Sunday night Jeff faced a crowd of youthful faces that betrayed the signs of their time—some eager, some jaded, some cynical, and others alternately defiant or questioning. As a youth pastor, Jeff strived to teach the teenagers in his care how to chart a godly course through a dark world of sex, drugs, and rock 'n' roll. At times the task seemed overwhelming, and he often felt unfit for the job as he shuffled to the parking lot after the meetings.

One night his head pastor took Jeff aside after the youth meeting. Looking him in the eye, he told Jeff what a difference he was making with the kids, how many of them seemed to respond to his nonintimidating leadership, and the approval of several parents in the congregation. The pastor reminded Jeff of everything he was doing right and gave him some timely counsel. Starting the next week, he suggested, why not appoint two or three teenage group leaders to work with small pockets of their peers in get-real sessions—times of prayer, reading the Bible, and sharing hurts and needs. Jeff would circulate among the groups offering leadership; the kids would get to know each other better and gradually drop their walls of defense.

After three months of get-real sessions Jeff stopped by the pastor's office one night. He thanked him for being a wise mentor and for investing in his life as a youth leader. Wisdom sets godly leadership apart from the pack.

I Will

Regard wisdom as a priceless treasure, worthy of possessing. _____ yes _____ no

Allow myself to grow in wisdom and grace through the years of my leadership. _____ yes _____ no

View mistakes as opportunities to grow. _____ yes _____ no

Look for ways to impart wisdom to those I lead. _____ yes _____ no

Expect God to bless me with the wisdom that I seek. _____ yes _____ no

When it comes to wisdom, I will examine my own heart more than I examine the hearts of others. _____ yes _____ no

Make the gaining of wisdom a primary goal in life. _____ yes _____ no

Things to Do

☐ *Read the book of Proverbs and tally how often it mentions wisdom.*

☐ *Find a proverb that has personal meaning for you, write it down, and post it where you'll see it daily.*

☐ *Think of an area in which you would like to improve, and seek the wisdom of a mentor about it.*

☐ *Look for opportunities to share with others the wisdom you've gained in leadership.*

☐ *Ask God to give you wisdom.*

☐ *Ask your mentor to share a story about how he/she gained wisdom in leadership.*

Things to Remember

You desire honesty from the heart, so you can teach me to be wise in my inmost being.

PSALM 51:6 NLT

Solomon was brilliant. God had blessed him with insight and understanding.

1 KINGS 4:29 CEV

Blessed is the one who finds wisdom. Blessed is the one who gains understanding. Wisdom pays better than silver does. She earns more than gold does.

PROVERBS 3:13–14 NIRV

The fear of the LORD is the beginning of wisdom; all who follow his precepts have good understanding. To him belongs eternal praise.

PSALM 111:10 NIV

So teach us to number our days, that we may present to You a heart of wisdom.

PSALM 90:12 NASB

The life-giving Spirit of GOD will hover over him, the Spirit that brings wisdom and understanding, the Spirit that gives direction and builds strength, the Spirit that instills knowledge and Fear-of-GOD.

ISAIAH 11:2 THE MESSAGE

What is the price of experience? Do men buy it for a song? Or wisdom for a dance in the street? No, it is bought with the price of all the man hath, his house, his wife, his children.

—WILLIAM BLAKE

Time ripens all things; no man is born wise.

—MIGUEL DE CERVANTES

Contentment

Satisfaction Guaranteed

---

*[Paul wrote:] Not that I speak in regard to need, for I have
learned in whatever state I am, to be content.*

—PHILIPPIANS 4:11 NKJV

For the third season in a row, the philharmonic orchestra
under Kevin's leadership had a chance to compete on a
national level against the best in the business. The previous
two seasons had ended in disappointment, but Kevin tried to
raise his musicians' morale by reminding them it was an
honor simply to qualify for the top competition. All season
long he pushed them to rehearse with precision and to play
with their hearts, not just their hands. When the day of the
competition arrived, they took their positions onstage and
played more beautifully than Kevin had ever heard them play
before.

After the performance, the members of the orchestra
gathered in the wings, excited at the likely prospect of winning
the competition. But when the master of ceremonies finally
announced the winning orchestra from the podium, it was
another city—another symphony orchestra—whose name he
called.

Tempers flared among some of the musicians. It was

unfair, they cried, that they should have worked so hard for so long and so *obviously* played the best, yet still only come in second place. Kevin quietly stood to his feet and pulled a New Testament from his shirt pocket. Curious as to what would happen next, the musicians gave him their full attention as he read the apostle Paul's famous words: "Whatever is true, whatever is noble, whatever is right, whatever is pure, whatever is lovely, whatever is admirable—if anything is excellent or praiseworthy—think about such things . . . I have learned to be content whatever the circumstances. I know what it is to be in need, and I know what it is to have plenty. I have learned the secret of being content in any and every situation" (Philippians 4:8, 11–12 NIV).

Kevin's quiet show of contentment in that moment of flaring emotions was worth more than any lecture he could have given. Chastened, the musicians packed their instruments and boarded the chartered bus back to town. Though he never said another word about it, Kevin knew the incident at the competition made a lasting impression. All throughout that year, and into the next, the orchestra pulled together and played as a single musician. They seemed to recapture the joy of making music simply because they could. Their contentment brought unity.

Contentment is one of those character traits not easily faked. You earn it the slow, hard way, like respect—by living and learning and doing as Christ, and the apostle Paul, would do.

I Will

Dwell on what I have, not on what I don't have.   *yes*   *no*

Remember that contentment is a godly trait worth
cultivating in my character.   *yes*   *no*

Believe that God blesses me daily with little acts of
kindness and things that often go unnoticed.   *yes*   *no*

Be thankful for my life, just the way it is.   *yes*   *no*

Stop competing and start enjoying life.   *yes*   *no*

Realize that God withholds some blessings from my
life for very good reasons.   *yes*   *no*

Trust that God knows what I need and don't need.   *yes*   *no*

Things to Do

☐ *Compare the greener grass of another organization or ministry, and take note of how good your own sod is.*

☐ *Write a short list of things you don't have but wish you did (talents, material possessions, spiritual gifts).*

☐ *Ask God to review your list and give you the things He desires for you and withhold the things He doesn't.*

☐ *Find three big things to be thankful for today, and state them out loud in front of your bathroom mirror.*

☐ *Find a friend who will be your contentment accountability partner. Check in with them often.*

☐ *Every time you catch yourself complaining, drop a quarter in a jar. See how much you total by week's end, and try to reduce it next week.*

Things to Remember

Now godliness with contentment is great gain.

1 TIMOTHY 6:6 NKJV

Keep falsehood and lies far from me; give me neither poverty nor riches, but give me only my daily bread.

PROVERBS 30:8 NIV

Don't fall in love with money. Be satisfied with what you have. The Lord has promised that he will not leave us or desert us.

HEBREWS 13:5 CEV

A simple life in the Fear-of-GOD is better than a rich life with a ton of headaches.

PROVERBS 15:16 THE MESSAGE

It is better to have little and be right than to have much and be wrong.

PSALM 37:16 NCV

If they obey and serve Him, they shall spend their days in prosperity, and their years in pleasures.

JOB 36:11 NKJV

Contentment is a pearl of great price, and whoever procures it at the expense of ten thousand desires makes a wise and a happy purchase.

—JOHN BALGUY

Content makes poor men rich; discontentment makes rich men poor.

—BENJAMIN FRANKLIN

Leaving a Legacy

Lasting Value

The Lord said to Jehu, "Because you have done well in doing what is right in My sight, and have done to the house of Ahab all that was in My heart, your sons shall sit on the throne of Israel to the fourth generation."

—2 Kings 10:30 NKJV

David sat on the front row of seats, amazed at his nervousness as he waited for the company spokesperson to introduce him for the annual chairman's speech. The fast food chain he had founded in the 1970s started as little more than a college whim, but over the years it had grown into one of the top fast food chains in the world. Now here he was, a man grown older and wiser and richer—in more ways than one.

Early on, David realized the importance of setting your standards high and sticking to them. His greatest challenge came when the other top chains started opening for business on Sundays. Competition in the fast food market was cutthroat, and his closest company advisers warned that if he didn't follow suit, the chain would fall behind in revenues and popularity—possibly starting a snowball effect.

David weighed the advice carefully and then turned to his ultimate source. He asked God what he should do. In the end, an obscure verse in the Bible about a king named Jehu swayed his heart—his chain would honor the Sabbath and remain closed for business.

The applause thundered in his ears as David realized the spokesperson had just called his name. He walked to the podium and waited for the cheering to die down. His topic for the speech was "Leaving a Legacy." Clearing his throat, he told the group about a young man who faced a crucial business decision early in his career, and that one decision had set the course for the entire company, as well as the hundreds of people it employed. As his retirement approached, David implored the company executives to carry high the torch that had been lighted three decades earlier. The crowd erupted into applause again and stood to their feet. In the seconds before he stepped down from the podium, David blinked back tears. God had indeed imprinted this company and used him to leave a lasting legacy.

The pages of Scripture and human history tell a recurring theme: What you do in this lifetime leaves tracks in the sand. Your legacy outlives you, for good or ill. What type of legacy you leave all depends on the choices you make today, and the next day, and the next. A person rarely jumps off the track of righteous living in one great leap. Instead, they veer off track gradually, almost imperceptibly, until one day they realize they are far from the place they started from.

Another David, the famous shepherd king of ancient Israel, is the only person whom the Bible says "had a heart after God." Can you imagine a more humbling—and awe-inspiring—descriptor? Try falling from that pedestal! (Later, of course, David did, but even then God restored him.) Early in his life David determined to follow the God of his father, and he took seriously the call to lead the Lord's people, Israel. Unlike his predecessor, King Saul, David chose God's ways above his own and sought alone times with his Lord. He established a powerful kingdom and left a godly legacy to his son Solomon.

What about you? Do the people you lead look to you for a righteous standard, a godly plumb line? Do they know you will always choose the ethical path when the lines between black and white are blurred? Perhaps without realizing it, every single day you carve another notch in your leadership legacy. Someday those you leave behind will face their own choice, to follow in your footsteps or to cut their own path. Again, history shows a strong propensity for like to follow like. In other words, the type of leadership you model is most likely the type of leadership you will spawn.

You may have failed in the past; you may have failed today. Don't fret about that. Give your failures to God, and move on with the calling He gave you.

I Will

Commit to leave a legacy of godliness in my
organization.

yes ___ _no_ ___

Keep the ethical high road top-of-mind in all my
decisions.

yes ___ _no_ ___

View failure or setbacks as opportunities to learn,
and then go on with God.

yes ___ _no_ ___

Take my responsibility as a role model for others
seriously.

yes ___ _no_ ___

Trust that God will help me on my quest to live
righteously.

yes ___ _no_ ___

Things to Do

☐ *Sketch out a legacy mission statement of what you want to be
remembered for in your organization.*

☐ *Find a mentor who exemplifies the godly legacy, and learn from them.*

☐ *Memorize Proverbs 10:7 (NIV)—"The memory of the righteous will be a
blessing, but the name of the wicked will rot."*

☐ *Ask God to help you make choices today that will have lasting value
years from now.*

☐ *Distill your leadership motto to one sentence, and write it down for
future leaders to follow.*

☐ *Find a young leader you can mentor, and model godly leadership
for them.*

Things to Remember

According to the grace of God which was given to me, as a wise master builder I have laid the foundation, and another builds on it. But let each one take heed how he builds on it.

1 CORINTHIANS 3:10 NKJV

Tell your children about it, let your children tell their children, and their children another generation.

JOEL 1:3 NKJV

In the same way, let your light shine before men, that they may see your good deeds and praise your Father in heaven.
Matthew 5:16 NIV

But continue thou in the things which thou hast learned and hast been assured of, knowing of whom thou hast learned them.

2 TIMOTHY 3:14 KJV

"Listen to me, all who hope for deliverance—all who seek the LORD! Consider the quarry from which you were mined, the rock from which you were cut!"

ISAIAH 51:1 NLT

God, we have heard what you did. Those who came before us have told us what you did in their days, in days long ago.

PSALM 44:1 NIRV

No man shall be able to stand before you all the days of your life; as I was with Moses, so I will be with you. I will not leave you nor forsake you.

JOSHUA 1:5 NKJV

It shall not be so among you; but whoever desires to become great among you shall be your servant.

MARK 10:43 NKJV

All of us! Nothing between us and God, our faces shining with the brightness of his face. And so we are transfigured much like the Messiah, our lives gradually becoming brighter and more beautiful as God enters our lives and we become like him.

2 CORINTHIANS 3:18 THE MESSAGE

If these things are yours and abound, you will be neither barren nor unfruitful in the knowledge of our Lord Jesus Christ

2 PETER 1:8 NKJV

In this you greatly rejoice, though now for a little while you may have had to suffer grief in all kinds of trials. These have come so that your faith—of greater worth than gold, which perishes even though refined by fire—may be proved genuine and may result in praise, glory and honor when Jesus Christ is revealed.

1 PETER 1:6–7 NIV

No legacy is so rich as honesty.

—WILLIAM SHAKESPEARE

Inventories can be managed, but people must be led.

—H. ROSS PEROT

Rest

Time Out

Rest in the LORD, and wait patiently for Him; do not fret because of him who prospers in his way, because of the man who brings wicked schemes to pass.

—PSALM 37:7 NKJV

In today's frenetic world, taking time out is something you have to schedule into your calendar or else it likely won't happen.

Victoria discovered how important times of respite are after three years of working nonstop on her Web-design business. As a new entrepreneur, she decided to throw herself headlong into the work to make a name for her company. The Internet market was so crowded with service providers that she feared she would miss out on potential business if she took a break. But after a near physical meltdown, her staff of three Web designers encouraged her to take a long-overdue vacation. If she pushed herself any harder, they warned, she might not be around to head up the company she'd worked so hard to make successful.

Before Victoria left town, a female staff member pulled her aside and offered to pray for her. She asked God to restore Victoria's vitality and enthusiasm for the work, as well as refresh her spirit during her time away.

"Don't worry," the staff member said as Victoria turned reluctantly to go. "We'll mind the fort. No phone calls or e-mails. Just rest."

Two weeks later, Victoria returned feeling like a new person. Her staff noticed the difference immediately. Gone were the worry lines that had etched her forehead, and she seemed lighthearted instead of edgy and intense.

You won't always have the luxury of taking time off when you want it, but schedule periodic time-outs and vacations whenever you can. Leaders who are rested in spirit, mind, and body perform at their peak and inspire a sense of balance in those they lead.

Jesus knew how crucial it was to get away from the crowds and the constant stress of ministry for time alone. He viewed solitude as an opportunity for recharging His physical and spiritual battery. Not only did He take time off, but He refused to allow Himself a guilt trip over doing it.

As you plan your leadership activities for the coming weeks and months, be sure to schedule in some time out. In the long run, those times of refreshing will make you a better leader, and those you lead will thank you for it.

I Will

Appreciate the physical, mental, and spiritual benefits of taking time out to rest.

_____ yes   _____ no

Protect my scheduled time off from the intrusion of other activities.

_____ yes   _____ no

Learn to take minibreaks, especially when I can't get away for a vacation.

_____ yes   _____ no

Determine to have a life and not just a career.

_____ yes   _____ no

Seek God's input on how I schedule my days.

_____ yes   _____ no

Trust God's promise to give rest to the weary and to renew my strength.

_____ yes   _____ no

Reflect on what it means to live a life of rest in the midst of busyness.

_____ yes   _____ no

Things to Do

☐ *Sometime this week, schedule a quiet time when you can do nothing. Write "Do Nothing" on your planner.*

☐ *Take all your vacation and holiday time this year.*

☐ *Make a priority of getting enough sleep and exercise to keep your body and mind healthy.*

☐ *Contrast the effect stress has on your body, mind, and spirit to that of a purpose-filled life with periods of rest built in.*

☐ *Look at your planner for this week. If it's overcrowded, eliminate or reschedule items that are nonessential.*

☐ *Allow yourself the luxury of a full recovery the next time you are sick.*

Things to Remember

"Come to me, all you who are weary and burdened, and I will give you rest."

MATTHEW 11:28 NIV

Though Zion is in ruins, the LORD will bring comfort, and the city will be as lovely as the garden of Eden that he provided. Then Zion will celebrate; it will be thankful and sing joyful songs.

ISAIAH 51:3 CEV

Thus says the LORD, "Stand by the ways and see and ask for the ancient paths, where the good way is, and walk in it; and you will find rest for your souls."

JEREMIAH 6:16 NASB

There is still a Sabbath rest for God's people. God rested from his work. Those who enjoy God's rest also rest from their work.

HEBREWS 4:9–10 NIrV

Now I can rest again, for the LORD has been so good to me.

PSALM 116:7 NLT

[The Lord] said, "My Presence will go with you, and I will give you rest."

EXODUS 33:14 NKJV

Every now and then go away, have a little relaxation, for when you come back to your work your judgment will be surer. Go some distance away because then the work appears smaller and more of it can be taken in at a glance and a lack of harmony and proportion is more readily seen.

—LEONARDO DA VINCI

No rest is worth anything except the rest that is earned.

—JEAN PAUL

Success

Right Action, Right Time

In every work that he began in the service of the house of God, in the law and in the commandment, to seek his God, he did it with all his heart. So he prospered.

—2 CHRONICLES 31:21 NKJV

If success in life could be packaged and sold for a fee, the purveyors could name their price and still have a steady stream of customers. Every leader secretly yearns to be successful, to make a difference in the organization or group they lead. But how you go about seeking success makes all the difference in the world. According to the Bible, the prescription for success is simple: to seek God and serve Him with all your heart. Or, as Jesus rendered it, "Seek first his kingdom and his righteousness, and all these things will be given to you as well" (Matthew 6:33 NIV). Contrast the following two leaders and the paths they took.

Bill set up shop in a busy strip mall near a competing store and practiced the dog-eat-dog method of retailing. He bad-mouthed the competition and worked his staff to the point of burnout, dangling the carrot of long-hours-equals-more-pay before them. Sometimes his ads bordered on making false claims, but Bill justified the practice by telling himself the ads brought in more customers. He even stole employees from his chief competitor and gloated over it.

Dan found an ideal location for his new bookstore and celebrated with a grand opening. When another bookstore opened in the area, he visited the store to contrast its strengths and weaknesses with his own. He noted that the other store was strong in travel and novelty books while he carried more self-help and religion titles. Dan asked the store owner if he would engage in some creative cross-marketing so that each business would benefit. Ironically, the two booksellers became friends, and instead of encroaching on each other's sales they actually improved them.

Soon Dan discovered that several churches in the area sought creative ways to draw in the singles crowd. He offered to host meet-and-greets in his café and eventually brought in speakers, musicians, and other entertainers to enhance the events. He paid percentage kickbacks anytime the other bookseller referred customers to him that resulted in a sale. That year the community voted the bookstores as the top two "cool hangout places" for the books-and-music crowd. Best of all, Dan watched relationships form and lives get touched spiritually in his bookstore café. He couldn't imagine work any more rewarding than what he was privileged to do.

When you lead God's way, taking care of the needs of others, God sees to it that your needs are covered as well. Look for ways to be a leader who puts the kingdom first; the Lord will add "all the rest" to your life.

I Will

	yes	no
Begin to see success through God's eyes.	_yes_	_no_
Remember that true success is not defined by dollars or numbers.	_yes_	_no_
Look to Christ as my model of successful leadership.	_yes_	_no_
Be thankful for the gifts and talents God has given me.	_yes_	_no_
Realize that every time I take care of the kingdom, God will take care of me.	_yes_	_no_
Serve others because I genuinely care for them, not just to gain brownie points.	_yes_	_no_
Remember that success tomorrow requires right action today.	_yes_	_no_

Things to Do

☐ *Ask God to be your source of success today.*

☐ *Read* The Wounded Healer *by Henri Nouwen on making life meaningful through the giving of yourself.*

☐ *Compliment a colleague on something he or she is consistently successful at.*

☐ *Reread Matthew 6 and jot down key verbs such as give, store up, and seek to help you remember its message.*

☐ *Look for an opportunity to help someone succeed at something this week.*

☐ *Think of ways you have grown in your quest for godly success, and write them down.*

Things to Remember

O LORD, save us; O LORD, grant us success.

PSALM 118:25 NIV

Counsel is mine, and sound wisdom; I am understanding, I have strength.

PROVERBS 8:14 NKJV

"Therefore, obey the terms of this covenant so that you will prosper in everything you do."

DEUTERONOMY 29:9 NLT

A grasping person stirs up trouble, but trust in GOD brings a sense of well-being.

PROVERBS 28:25 THE MESSAGE

If you don't sharpen your ax, it will be harder to use; if you are smart, you'll know what to do.

ECCLESIASTES 10:10 CEV

The Lord said, "Who then is that faithful and wise steward, whom his master will make ruler over his household, to give them their portion of food in due season? Blessed is that servant whom his master will find so doing when he comes. Truly, I say to you that he will make him ruler over all that he has.

LUKE 12:42–44 NKJV

The person who tries to live alone will not succeed as a human being. His heart withers if it does not answer another heart. His mind shrinks away if he hears only the echoes of his own thoughts and finds no other inspiration.

—PEARL S. BUCK

The person who goes farthest is generally the one who is willing to do and dare. The sure-thing boat never gets far from shore.

—DALE CARNEGIE

Books in the Checklist for Life series

Checklist for Life
ISBN 0-7852-6455-8

Checklist for Life for Graduates
ISBN 0-7852-6186-9

Checklist for Life for Leaders
ISBN 0-7852-6001-3

Checklist for Life for Teens
ISBN 0-7852-6461-2

Checklist for Life for Women
ISBN 0-7852-6462-0

Checklist for Life for Men
ISBN 0-7852-6463-9